PRAISE FOR *THE EMPATH'S SURVIVAL GUIDE*

"Have you ever been told that you need to grow a thicker skin? Do you suspect that your sensitivity is the source not only of your pain but also of your joy, plus your empathy, creativity, and spirituality besides? This is the book for you. Written with—what else?—tremendous empathy, *The Empath's Survival Guide* will help you to understand yourself and your gifts, and to forge a healthy path through this ever-coarsening but deeply beautiful world."

SUSAN CAIN
New York Times bestselling author of *Quiet*
and founder of Quiet Revolution

"Dr. Orloff combines neuroscience, intuition, and energy medicine to show you how to stay powerful and strong in the world, while also keeping your compassion and empathy alive."

DEEPAK CHOPRA
author of *Super Genes*

"*The Empath's Survival Guide* is wonderful, warm, and wise. Reading Judith's book is like having a very savvy sister who teaches you the insider skills of how to deal with this perplexing and amazing talent of extreme sensitivity. We all know someone who is extremely sensitive, and the world hits them hard. It could be you, your sister or brother, your spouse, a coworker, or a friend. This book is packed with practical hints for embracing sensitivity and turning it into a gift."

LORIN ROCHE
author of *The Radiance Sutras*

"Being an empath is the new normal—and what a perfect guide-book. Now people will know how to cope with being highly sensitive in their everyday lives. Fabulous and so timely. Everyone needs this book."

"In this groundbreaking book, Dr. Judith Orloff provides us with a deep understanding of the empath's journey. Her professional knowledge, as well as her personal experience as an empath—combined with the practical tools for surviving in a sometimes challenging world—make her the leading expert in the field. This book will not only help you to cope with being a sensitive person, it will teach you how to tune your abilities and develop a coherent set of skills to master yourself. Dr. Orloff does a brilliant job in helping us discover the empath in all of us."

"Dr. Orloff has done a great service to empaths everywhere with *The Empath's Survival Guide*. This information will help thousands of people protect themselves from psychic vampires, set healthy boundaries, and recognize their sensitivity as the gift it truly is."

"This book is essential reading for anyone who feels overwhelmed by our chaotic world and wants to master tools to become a more sensitive, whole, and powerful person. It's also for the loved ones of sensitive people who want to understand them better. It is easy to read, straight to the point, and offers practical ways for loving people to thrive and avoid compassion burnout. A physician and empath herself, Dr. Orloff shows you how to prevent sensory overload by setting healthy boundaries with many types of draining people, including narcissists. This book is a lifetime guide to return to again and again. Highly recommended!"

JOAN BORYSENKO, PHD
author of *New York Times* bestseller
Minding the Body, Mending the Mind

"*The Empath's Survival Guide* is a lifesaver for sensitive people and anyone who wants to become more empathic in their relationships without taking on your partner's stress. Highly recommended!"

JOHN GRAY, PHD
author of the international bestseller
Men Are from Mars, Women Are from Venus

"Once in a while a book appears that could have described yet another pathology. Instead *The Empath's Survival Guide* by Judith Orloff humanizes a group of persons whose special traits and talents are normalized on the continuum of human experience and appreciated for their specialness. We recommend everyone read this book to broaden their view of human diversity and deepen their empathy for special talents and challenges."

HARVILLE HENDRIX, PHD, and HELEN LAKELLY HUNT, PHD
coauthors of the *New York Times* bestseller *Getting the Love You Want, Imago Relationship Therapy*, and *Making Marriage Simple*

"Anyone feeling too stressed or too sensitive to personal or planetary changes will love this new book. It provides tips, tools, and techniques for those of us often misunderstood by others. A masterpiece of love and understanding."

JOE VITALE
author of *Zero Limits* and *The Attractor Factor*

"Many individuals discover that opening to others through love, compassion, and empathy involves becoming vulnerable and often damaged psychologically and spiritually. Empaths, take heart! The solution is not to give up empathy, but to develop skills that avoid being damaged or blindsided in the process. Dr. Judith Orloff's *The Empath's Survival Guide* shows how. This book is seriously needed. It addresses an issue long ignored in healing, psychology, and medicine."

LARRY DOSSEY, MD
author of *One Mind: How Our Individual Mind Is Part of a Greater Consciousness and Why It Matters*

THE
EMPATH'S
SURVIVAL
GUIDE

BOOKS AND AUDIO PROGRAMS
BY JUDITH ORLOFF, MD

Books

The Power of Surrender: Let Go and Energize Your Relationships, Success, and Well-Being

Emotional Freedom: Liberate Yourself from Negative Emotions and Transform Your Life

Positive Energy: 10 Extraordinary Prescriptions for Transforming Fatigue, Stress, and Fear into Vibrance, Strength, and Love

Second Sight: An Intuitive Psychiatrist Tells Her Extraordinary Story and Shows You How to Tap Your Own Inner Wisdom

Dr. Judith Orloff's Guide to Intuitive Healing: 5 Steps to Physical, Emotional, and Sexual Wellness

Audio

Essential Tools for Empaths: A Survival Guide for Sensitive People

The Ecstasy of Letting Go: Surrender Practices to Empower Your Life

Emotional Freedom Practices: How to Transform Difficult Emotions into Positive Energy

Becoming an Intuitive Healer: A Professional Development Course for Health Practitioners

Positive Energy Practices: How to Attract Uplifting People and Combat Energy Vampires

Awakening Second Sight: Emergence of a Medical Doctor's Psychic Ability

JUDITH ORLOFF, MD

THE EMPATH'S SURVIVAL GUIDE

Life Strategies *for* Sensitive People

sounds true
BOULDER, COLORADO

Sounds True
Boulder, CO 80306

Published 2017

Book design by Beth Skelley

Printed in Canada

Library of Congress Cataloging-in-Publication Data
Names: Orloff, Judith, author.
Title: The empath's survival guide : life strategies for sensitive people /
    Judith Orloff, MD.
Description: Boulder, Colorado : Sounds True, Inc., [2017] |
    Includes bibliographical references and index.
Identifiers: LCCN 2016032679 (print) | LCCN 2016042066 (ebook) |
    ISBN 9781622036578 (hardcover) | ISBN 9781622038312 (ebook)
Subjects: LCSH: Sensitivity (Personality trait) | Self-actualization (Psychology)
Classification: LCC BF698.35.S47 O75 2017 (print) |
    LCC BF698.35.S47 (ebook) | DDC 155.2—dc23
LC record available at https://lccn.loc.gov/2016032679

10 9 8 7 6 5 4 3 2 1

For Corey Folsom

CONTENTS

Our innate capacity for empathy is the source
of the most precious of all human qualities.

His Holiness the 14th Dalai Lama

Chapter 1

ARE YOU AN EMPATH?
Introduction to Empathy

I'm a physician with fourteen years of conventional medical training at USC and UCLA. I am also an empath. In my medical practice of over two decades, I specialize in treating highly sensitive people like myself. Though there is a spectrum of sensitivity that exists in human beings, empaths are emotional sponges who absorb both the stress and joy of the world. We feel everything, often to an extreme, and have little guard up between others and ourselves. As a result, we are often overwhelmed by excessive stimulation and are prone to exhaustion and sensory overload.

I'm so passionate about this topic both professionally and personally because I've had to develop specific strategies to manage the challenges of being an empath myself. These allow me to protect my sensitivities so I can maximize their benefits—and there are *so* many! I want to share with you how to become a balanced, empowered, and happy empath. To thrive, you must learn ways to avoid taking on the energy, symptoms, and stress of others. I also want to educate your loved ones and peers—family, coworkers, bosses, parents, and romantic partners—on how best to support and communicate with you. In this book, I will show you how to accomplish these goals.

I offer *The Empath's Survival Guide* as a resource for kindred sensitive souls to find understanding and acceptance in a world that is often coarse, heartless, and disdainful of sensitivity. In it, I challenge the status quo and create a new normal for how to view sensitivity, wherever you are on the spectrum. There is nothing "wrong" with being sensitive. In fact, you are about to discover what's most "right" about yourself. Through this book, its companion audio program, *Essential Tools for Empaths*, and my workshops for empaths, I want to create a community of support so that you can find your tribe, be authentic, and shine. I want to support a movement of people who honor their sensitivities. Welcome to a circle of love! My message to you is one of hope and acceptance. I encourage you to embrace your gifts and manifest your full power on the empath journey.

WHAT IS AN EMPATH?

Empaths have an extremely reactive neurological system. We don't have the same filters that other people do to block out stimulation. As a consequence, we absorb into our own bodies both the positive and stressful energies around us. We are so sensitive that it's like holding something in a hand that has fifty fingers instead of five. We are truly super responders.

Research shows that high sensitivity affects approximately 20 percent of the population, though the degree of one's sensitivity can vary.[1] Empaths have often been labeled as "overly sensitive" and told to "get a thicker skin." As children and adults, we are shamed for our sensitivities rather than supported. We may experience chronic exhaustion and want to retreat from the world because it often feels so overwhelming. But at this point in my life, I wouldn't give up being an empath for anything.

It lets me sense the secrets of the universe and know passion beyond my wildest dreams.

However, my empathic abilities haven't always felt this incredible to me.

GROWING UP AS AN EMPATH

Like many empathic children, I never fit in. In fact, I felt like an alien on earth waiting to be transported to my real home in the stars. I remember sitting in my front yard looking up at the universe and hoping that a spaceship would take me home. I was an only child, so I spent a lot of time by myself. I had no one to relate to who could understand my sensitivities. No one seemed to be like me. My parents, who were both physicians—I come from a family of twenty-five physicians—said, "Sweetheart, toughen up and get a thicker skin," which I didn't want or even know how to do. I couldn't go to crowded malls or parties. I'd walk in feeling fine and walk out exhausted, dizzy, anxious, or suffering from some ache or pain I didn't have before.

What I didn't know back then was that everyone has a subtle energy field surrounding their body, a subtle radiant light that penetrates and extends beyond it a distance of inches or even feet. These fields communicate information such as emotions and physical well-being or distress. When we are in crowded places, the energy fields of others overlap with ours. I picked up all of these intense sensations, but I had absolutely no idea what they were or how to interpret them. I just felt anxious and tired in crowds. And most of all, I wanted to escape.

As a teenager in Los Angeles, I got heavily involved with drugs to block out my sensitivities. (I'm not recommending this to you!) Then, with my sensitivities numbed, I could cope. I was able to attend parties and hang out at shopping malls, just like my friends, and would feel fine. What a relief that was! In my memoir, *Second Sight,* I wrote about how I turned to drugs to shut off my intuition and empathic abilities. But after a near-tragic car accident, during which I went over a 1,500-foot cliff in Topanga Canyon at three in the morning in an Austin Mini Cooper, my parents were scared to death and sent me to a psychiatrist.

Naturally, I fought my psychiatrist the whole way. But, in fact, this angel in human form was the first person to help me realize that to become whole I had to embrace my sensitivities, not run from them. This was the start of my healing and self-acceptance as an empath. Since I was so frightened by my childhood empathic and intuitive experiences, part of my evolution as a physician and a woman has been to learn to embrace these abilities. They are precious and deserve to be nurtured and supported. That's why I specialize in helping empaths in my psychiatric practice and workshops.

> IF YOU FEEL AS IF YOU DON'T FIT INTO THIS WORLD, IT'S BECAUSE YOU'RE HERE TO CREATE A BETTER ONE.
>
> **Author Unknown**

Yes, we empaths *can* flourish! Empathy is the medicine the world needs.

THE EMPATH EXPERIENCE

Now let's explore in more detail the empath experience. See if you relate personally or have a loved one or colleague who qualifies as an empath.

First, what is the difference between ordinary empathy and being an empath? Ordinary empathy means our heart goes out to another person when they are going through a difficult period. It also means that we can be happy for others during their times of joy. As an empath, however, we actually sense other people's emotions, energy, and physical symptoms in our bodies, without the usual filters that most people have. We can experience other people's sorrow and also their joy. We are supersensitive to their tone of voice and body movements. We can hear what they don't say in words but communicate nonverbally and through silence. Empaths feel things first, *then* think, which is the opposite of how most people function in our overintellectualized society. There is no membrane that separates us from the world. This makes us very different from other people who have had their defenses up almost from the time they were born.

Empaths share some or all of the traits of what psychologist Elaine Aron calls Highly Sensitive People, or HSPs. These traits include a low threshold for stimulation, the need for alone time, sensitivity to light, sound, and smell, plus an aversion to large groups. In addition, it takes highly sensitive people longer to wind down after a busy day because their system's ability to transition from high stimulation to quiet and calm is slower. Empaths also share a highly sensitive person's love of nature and quiet environments.

Empaths, however, take the experience of the highly sensitive person further. We can sense subtle energy, which is called *shakti* or *prana* in Eastern healing traditions, and we absorb this energy into our own bodies. Highly sensitive people don't typically do that. This capacity allows us to experience the energies around us in extremely deep ways. Since everything is made of subtle energy, including emotions and physical sensations, we energetically internalize the feelings, pain, and various physical sensations of others. We often have trouble distinguishing someone else's discomfort from our own. Also, some empaths have profound spiritual and intuitive experiences, which aren't usually associated with highly sensitive people. Some empaths are even able to communicate with animals, nature, and their inner guides. But being a highly sensitive person and an empath are not mutually exclusive: you can be both at the same time.

To determine if you are an empath, see if you relate to one or more of these types.

GENERAL TYPES OF EMPATHS

Physical Empaths. You are especially attuned to other people's physical symptoms and tend to absorb them into your body. You also can become energized by someone's sense of well-being.

Emotional Empaths. You mainly pick up other people's emotions and can become a sponge for their feelings, both happy and sad.

Intuitive Empaths. You experience extraordinary perceptions such as heightened intuition, telepathy, messages in dreams, animal and plant communication, as well as contact with the Other Side. The following includes the different types and how they function:

- **Telepathic Empaths** receive intuitive information about others in present time.

- **Precognitive Empaths** have premonitions about the future while awake or dreaming.

- **Dream Empaths** are avid dreamers and can receive intuitive information from dreams that helps others and guides them in their own lives.

- **Mediumship Empaths** can access spirits on the Other Side.

- **Plant Empaths** can feel the needs of plants and connect with their essence.

- **Earth Empaths** are attuned to changes in our planet, our solar system, and the weather.

- **Animal Empaths** can tune in to animals and communicate with them.

Empaths have diverse and beautifully nuanced sensitivities. You may be one or more of the above types. In future chapters, I'll also discuss specific kinds of physical and emotional empaths, such as food empaths (who are attuned to the energy of foods) and relationship and sexual empaths (who are attuned to their partners' and friends' moods, sensuality, and physical health). As you learn to identify your special talents, you will find they can not only enrich your life but also be used for the good of others.

STYLES OF RELATING: INTROVERTED AND EXTROVERTED EMPATHS

Physical, emotional, and intuitive empaths can have different styles of socializing and interacting with the world. Most empaths are introverted, though some are extroverted. Other empaths are a combination of both. Introverted empaths, like me, have a minimal tolerance for socializing and small talk. They tend to be quieter at gatherings and prefer leaving early. Often they arrive in their own cars so they don't have to feel trapped or dependent on others for a ride.

> MANY EMPATHS DON'T LIKE SMALL TALK. IT EXHAUSTS THEM.
>
> Judith Orloff, MD

I love my close circle of friends and mostly stay away from big parties or gatherings. I also don't like small talk, and I've never learned to do it, which is common for the introverted type. I can socialize in groups for usually two to three hours before I feel overstimulated. My friends all know this about me and don't take it personally when I excuse myself early.

In contrast, extroverted empaths are more verbal and interactive when socializing and enjoy the banter with others more than introverted empaths do. They also can stay longer in social situations without getting exhausted or overstimulated.

HOW DOES SOMEONE BECOME AN EMPATH?

Many factors can contribute. Some babies enter the world with more sensitivity than others—an inborn temperament. You can actually *see* it when they come out of the womb.

They're much more responsive to light, smells, touch, movement, temperature, and sound. Also, from what I've observed with my patients and workshop participants, some sensitivity may be genetically transmitted. Highly sensitive children can come from mothers and fathers with the same traits. In addition, parenting plays a role. Childhood neglect or abuse can also affect sensitivity levels for adults. A portion of empaths I've treated have experienced early trauma, such as emotional or physical abuse, or were raised by alcoholic, depressed, or narcissistic parents. This could potentially wear down the usual healthy defenses that a child with nurturing parents develops. As a result of their upbringing, these children typically don't feel "seen" by their families, and they also feel invisible in the greater world that doesn't value sensitivity. In all cases, however, empaths haven't learned to defend against stress in the same way others have. We're different in this respect. A noxious stimulus, such as an angry person, crowds, noise, or bright light, can agitate us because our threshold for sensory overload is extremely low.

THE SCIENCE OF EMPATHY

There are a number of scientific findings explaining the empath experience that I find fascinating.

The Mirror Neuron System

Researchers have discovered a specialized group of brain cells that are responsible for compassion. These cells enable everyone to mirror emotions, to share another person's pain, fear, or joy. Because empaths are thought to have hyperresponsive mirror neurons, we deeply resonate with other people's feelings.

How does this occur? Mirror neurons are triggered by outside events. For example, when our spouse gets hurt, we feel hurt too. When our child is crying, we feel sad as well, and when our friend is happy, we also feel happy. In contrast, psychopaths, sociopaths, and narcissists are thought to have what science calls "empathy deficient disorders" (see chapter 5). This means they lack the ability to feel empathy the way other people do, which may be caused by an underactive mirror neuron system. We must beware of these people because they are incapable of unconditional love.[2]

Electromagnetic Fields

The second finding is based on the fact that both the brain and the heart generate electromagnetic fields. According to the HeartMath Institute, these fields transmit information about people's thoughts and emotions. Empaths may be particularly sensitive to this input and tend to become overwhelmed by it. Similarly, we often have stronger physical and emotional responses to changes in the electromagnetic fields of the earth and the sun. Empaths know well that what happens to the earth and the sun affects our state of mind and energy.[3]

Emotional Contagion

The third finding that enhances our understanding of empaths is the phenomenon of emotional contagion. Research has shown that many people pick up the emotions of those around them. For instance, one crying infant will set off a wave of crying babies in a hospital ward. Or one person loudly expressing anxiety in the workplace can spread it to other workers. People commonly catch other people's feelings in groups. A recent article in the *New York Times* stated that this ability to synchronize moods with others is crucial for good relationships. What is the lesson for empaths? To choose positive people in our lives so that we're not brought down by negativity. And when a friend is going through a hard time, we need to take special precautions to ground and center ourselves. These are important strategies that you will learn in this book.[4]

Increased Dopamine Sensitivity

The fourth finding involves dopamine, a neurotransmitter that increases the activity of neurons and is associated with the pleasure response. Research has shown that introverted empaths tend to have a higher sensitivity to dopamine than extroverts. Basically, introverted empaths need less dopamine to feel happy. That could explain why they are more content with alone time, reading, and meditation and need less external stimulation from parties and other large social gatherings. In contrast, extroverts crave the dopamine rush they get from lively events. In fact, they often can't get enough of it.[5]

Synesthesia

The fifth finding, which I find particularly compelling, is the extraordinary state called "mirror-touch synesthesia." Synesthesia is a neurological condition in which two different senses are paired in the brain—for instance, seeing colors when you hear a piece of music or tasting words. Famous synesthetics include Isaac Newton, Billy Joel, and Itzhak Perlman. However, with mirror-touch synesthesia, people actually feel the emotions and sensations of others in their own bodies, as if these emotions were their own. This is a wonderful neurological explanation of an empath's experience.[6]

WHAT AREAS OF LIFE
DOES EMPATHY AFFECT?

Empathy can be present in the following areas of daily life:

- **Health.** Many of the empaths who come to me as patients and in my workshops feel overwhelmed, fatigued, and downright exhausted before they learn practical skills to help them cope with their sensitivities. They have often been diagnosed with agoraphobia, chronic fatigue, fibromyalgia, migraines, chronic pain, allergies, and adrenal fatigue (a form of burnout). On an emotional level, they may experience anxiety, depression, or panic attacks. We will discuss all of these topics in chapter 2.

- **Addictions.** Some empaths become addicted to alcohol, drugs, food, sex, shopping, or other behaviors in an attempt to numb their sensitivities. Overeating is common since some empaths unwittingly use food to ground themselves. Empaths can easily become overweight because the extra padding provides protection from negative energy. In chapter 3, we'll look at healthier coping mechanisms.

- **Relationships, Love, and Sex.** Empaths may unknowingly get involved with toxic partners and become anxious, depressed, or ill. They give their hearts too easily to narcissists and other unavailable people. Empaths are loving and expect others to be that way, which doesn't always happen. They also absorb their partner's stress and emotions, such as anger or depression, simply by interacting with them, as well as during lovemaking—a particularly vulnerable time. In chapters 4 and 5, you'll learn how to have a healthy relationship without getting overloaded, as well as ways to set clear boundaries with toxic people in your life.

- **Parenting.** Empathic parents often feel especially overwhelmed and exhausted from the intense demands of child-rearing because they tend to absorb their children's feelings and pain. In chapter 6, empaths who are parents will learn skills to prevent them from doing this. In addition, empathic children can feel overwhelmed by their sensitivities. Their parents need a special education in helping these children to nurture their gifts and to thrive.

- **Work.** Empaths can feel drained by energy vampires in their workplace yet be at a loss to know how to set boundaries to protect themselves. In chapter 7, empaths will learn to center and replenish themselves in a work environment that may be excessively stimulating or have little privacy.

- **Extraordinary Perceptual Abilities.** Empaths have high sensitivities that can make them more intuitive, able to sense people's energy, and open to premonitions, animal communication, and powerful dreams. In chapter 8, we'll look at how they can become empowered by these abilities in a grounded way.

SELF-ASSESSMENT   **Are You an Empath?**

To find out, take the following empath self-assessment, answering "mostly yes" or "mostly no" to each question.

- Have I ever been labeled overly sensitive, shy, or introverted?

- Do I frequently get overwhelmed or anxious?

- Do arguments and yelling make me ill?

- Do I often feel like I don't fit in?

- Do crowds drain me, and do I need alone time to revive myself?

- Do noise, odors, or nonstop talkers overwhelm me?

- Do I have chemical sensitivities or a low tolerance for scratchy clothes?

- Do I prefer taking my own car to places so that I can leave early if I need to?

- Do I overeat to cope with stress?

- Am I afraid of becoming suffocated by intimate relationships?

- Do I startle easily?

- Do I react strongly to caffeine or medications?

- Do I have a low threshold for pain?

- Do I tend to socially isolate?

- Do I absorb other people's stress, emotions, or symptoms?

- Am I overwhelmed by multitasking, and do I prefer to do one thing at a time?

- Do I replenish myself in nature?

- Do I need a long time to recuperate after being with difficult people or energy vampires?
- Do I feel better in small cities or the country rather than large cities?
- Do I prefer one-to-one interactions and small groups to large gatherings?

Now calculate your results.

- If you answered yes to one to five questions, you're at least a partial empath.
- If you answered yes to six to ten questions, you have moderate empath tendencies.
- If you answered yes to eleven to fifteen questions, you have strong empath tendencies.
- If you answered yes to more than fifteen questions, you are a full-blown empath.

Determining to what degree you are an empath will clarify your needs and the strategies you must learn to meet them. This is essential to gain a comfort zone in your life.

ADVANTAGES AND CHALLENGES OF BEING AN EMPATH

Being an empath brings both advantages and challenges.

Common Advantages

I cherish being an empath. I'm grateful for the blessings my sensitivities bestow on me each day. I love being intuitive, feeling the flow of energy in the world, reading people, and experiencing the richness of being so open to life and nature.

We empaths have many marvelous traits. We have huge hearts and the instinct to help others in need or who are less fortunate. We're dreamers and idealists. We're also passionate, deep, creative, in touch with our emotions, compassionate, and can see the big picture. We can appreciate another's feelings and become loyal friends and mates. We're intuitive, spiritual, and can sense energy. We have a special appreciation for the natural world and feel at home there. We resonate with nature, its plants, forests, and gardens, and we often love water. Whether we are soaking in the womb-like, warm water of a bath or living by an ocean or a river, water energizes us. In addition, we may feel a strong intuitive bond with our animal companions. We often talk to them like they are humans, and we may become involved with animal rescue or animal communication.

Common Challenges

Once you begin to deal with the challenges of being an empath and gain more coping skills, you will *really* enjoy all the advantages. The common challenges I've known and seen with my patients and workshop participants include the following:

- **Becoming overstimulated.** Since you don't possess the same defenses as others, you may often feel like you have raw nerve endings and burn out easily. Without enough alone time to replenish yourself and wind down each day, you will suffer from the toxic effects of overstimulation and sensory overload.

- **Absorbing the stress and negativity of others.** Sometimes you can't tell if an emotion or sense of bodily discomfort is your own or someone else's. Taking on other people's distress can lead to a variety of physical and emotional symptoms in you, from pain to anxiety.

- **Feeling things intensely.** You may be unable to watch violent or upsetting movies about people or animals because the brutality hurts too much. You may carry the weight of the world on your shoulders, feeling the pain of others in your life or those you witness suffering in the news.

- **Experiencing emotional and social hangovers.** When you're around too many people or intense emotions, the malaise of sensory overload can linger long after the event.

- **Feeling isolated and lonely.** You may isolate yourself or keep yourself distant from people because the world seems so overwhelming. As a result, others may view you as standoffish. Like many empaths, you may be hypervigilant at scanning your environment to ensure it's safe, which others can perceive as a signal to stay away. You may also freeze around inauthentic people, which can convey aloofness—but this is clearly a protective device. Some empaths prefer socializing online to keep others at a distance, so there's less of the tendency to absorb their discomfort and stress.

- **Experiencing emotional burnout.** A downside of being so compassionate is that people flock to you to tell you their life stories. Ever since I was a child, it was as if I wore a sign saying, "I can help you." This is why empaths must set clear boundaries with others and not "overgive."

- **Coping with increased sensitivity to light, smell, taste, touch, temperature, and sound.** For many empaths, and myself, loud noises and bright lights are painful. They penetrate and shock our bodies. I hold my ears when an ambulance goes by. Hearing leaf blowers and loud machinery is jarring. I also can't tolerate the explosive blasts of fireworks. They startle me, and I react like a frightened dog reacts. Empaths have an enhanced startle response because we are super-responsive to intense sensory input. Strong smells and chemicals, such as exhaust and perfumes, make us feel queasy, allergic, or suffocated. We're also sensitive to temperature extremes and may dislike air-conditioning. Our bodies can be energized or depleted by intense weather, such as a thunderstorm, gusty winds, or a snowfall. Many empaths are energized by a bright full moon, while others are agitated by it.

- **Expressing needs in intimate relationships.** Empaths have specific needs when living in the same space or sharing a bed with someone. Many require a separate space and sometimes a separate bed to feel comfortable. It's important for empaths to have conversations with their partners about their specific needs.

Special Challenges for Each Gender

An empath's sensitivities can be challenging in different ways for men and women, though of course there is much overlap.

For instance, male empaths are often ashamed of their sensitivities and reluctant to talk about them. They may feel they're not "masculine enough." They have had to fight gender stereotypes and were probably warned not to be a "crybaby" and to "act like a man." Boys are taught that "strong men don't cry," and sensitive boys can be bullied at school for being "sissies." Male empaths may not be attracted to football, soccer, or aggressive contact sports, and so they may be excluded and shamed by the other boys. Consequently, male empaths may repress their emotions and eventually even forget they have them. For all these reasons, they often suffer in silence, which can negatively impact their relationships, careers, and health. Highly sensitive men who are famous include Abraham Lincoln, Albert Einstein, and Jim Carrey.

I find sensitive men incredibly attractive. I love Alanis Morissette's song "In Praise of the Vulnerable Man." To become well balanced, men must own their sensitive sides. I'm not talking about overly feminized men who have not learned to embody the masculine but rather balanced men who are strong enough to be sensitive and secure enough to be vulnerable. Such men have a high emotional IQ. They are not afraid of emotions, their own or another's. This makes them compassionate and attractive partners, friends, and leaders.

In contrast, female empaths in Western culture are given more permission to express their emotions and "female intuition," though by no means does our world embrace feminine power. Throughout much of history, the feminine has been squashed. Think of the Inquisition during the Dark Ages or the

Salem witch trials, where sensitives were burned at the stake. When I first started speaking about intuition to groups, I was afraid I would be harmed. But once I realized I was tuning in to the collective energy of women seers who had been suppressed over the ages, I discovered that today is a different time. It is much safer to express my voice now, so my discomfort has lifted.

Similarly, many of my female patients have been reluctant to authentically express their sensitivities for fear of being misunderstood, judged, or abandoned. It's important that we learn to be authentic in relationships about our empathic needs. Also, for some women empaths, empathy can turn into codependency. They have such big hearts that they get caught up in caretaking roles, attending to others more than they attend to themselves. A female empath who is balanced knows how to set boundaries with her time and energy. She learns to give and receive in a balanced way, a powerful combination. Female empaths who are famous include Nicole Kidman, Jewel (her song "Sensitive" is about empaths), Winona Ryder, Alanis Morissette, and Princess Diana.

> EMPATHS ARE NOT
> "OVERLY SENSITIVE."
> THEY HAVE A GIFT BUT
> MUST LEARN TO MANAGE
> THEIR SENSITIVITIES.
> Judith Orloff, MD

THRIVING AS AN EMPATH:
SKILLS TO PREVENT OVERLOAD

Throughout this book, I'll be sharing skills to help empaths manage the challenges and enhance the many advantages of their abilities. Although society may say empaths are "too sensitive" and suggest that we "toughen up," I encourage empaths to develop their sensitivities even more, while staying centered with them. Being an empath is a huge asset when you learn to manage it. Empaths are not crazy, neurotic, weak, or hypochondriacs. They are wonderful, sensitive people with a gift, but all of us need tools to cope.

A skill that sensitive people must learn is how to deal with sensory overload when too much is coming at them too quickly. This can leave them exhausted, anxious, depressed, or sick. Like many of us, you may feel there is no on/off switch for your empathy. This is *not* true. I'll show you how to take charge of your sensitivities rather than feeling victimized by them. When you feel protected and safe, the world will become your playground.

To gain a sense of safety, recognize some of the common factors that contribute to empathy overload. Once you begin to identify your triggers, you can quickly act to remedy a situation.

What makes an empath's overload symptoms worse? Fatigue, illness, rushing, traffic, crowds, loud environments, toxic people, low blood sugar, arguing, overwork, chemical sensitivities, too much socializing, and feeling trapped in overstimulating situations such as parties and cruises. Any combination of these conditions intensifies an empath's overload. Therefore, keep the following in mind: stress + low blood sugar = drama and exhaustion.

What makes an empath's overload symptoms better? When I experience sensory overload, I need to slow everything down and unplug from all stimulation. If it gets really intense, I feel like a flower that's wilting, and that's when I need sustenance from stillness. I often retreat to a room without sound or bright light, and I sleep or meditate to recalibrate myself at a lower level of stimulation. Sometimes solitude for an entire day or a weekend is necessary if my sensory overload is extreme. Still, during such times, I may take short walks out in nature and limit my trips out to take care of errands. The problem is that empaths often see things as "all or nothing." Either we're on the go or retreating to the safe haven of home. I suggest that you moderate this radical stance so that you can find balance and not suffer from undue isolation or loneliness. Listen to your intuition about what is right for you. Each of us has to find our own way in honoring our needs.

To deal with overload, a patient told me, "Only one-to-one contact with people is bearable. Groups just feel too intense." Yet another patient explained to me, "I decompress at night when everyone is sleeping and the whole world is resting. The invisible energetic buzz of the day quiets down, and I can relax and focus."

In addition, shielding is a basic skill I recommend to prevent empathic overload. Shielding is a quick way to protect yourself. Many empaths rely on it to block out toxic energy while still allowing for the free flow of positive energies. I suggest you regularly use this skill. The minute you're uncomfortable with a person, place, or situation, put up your shield. Use it in an airport, at a party if you're talking to an energy vampire, or in a packed doctor's waiting room. Shielding puts you in a safe bubble where you won't be drained.

PROTECTION STRATEGY
Shielding Visualization for Empaths

Allow at least five minutes for this exercise. Find a quiet and protected space. Make sure that you won't be interrupted. Loosen your clothing and find a position that's comfortable, perhaps sitting cross-legged on the floor or upright on a chair. Begin by taking a few deep, long breaths. Breathe in, really feeling the inhalation, and then exhale, really letting out a big exhalation. Feel the sensuality of the breath, the connection to prana, the sacred life force.

Let all thoughts drift by like clouds in the sky, returning to your breath over and over again to find your center. Feel a core of energy running from your toes, throughout your body, and up through the top of your head. Focusing on this will keep you centered.

In this relaxed state, visualize a beautiful shield of white or pink light surrounding your body completely and extending a few inches beyond it. This shield protects you from anything negative, stressful, toxic, or intrusive. Within the protection of the shield, feel yourself centered, happy, and energized. This shield blocks out negativity, though at the same time, you can still feel what is positive and loving. Get used to the sensation of the shield protecting your body. You can visualize the shield whenever you suspect you're absorbing someone else's energy.

To close, inwardly say "thank you" for this protection. Take a long, deep breath in and out, and then slowly open your eyes. Come back to the room. Be in your body 100 percent. ■

Along with shielding, daily self-care for empaths involves eating well and minimizing stress. In addition, certain actions are a balm for both body and soul. These include taking quiet alone time, associating with positive people, being in nature, immersing yourself in water to clear negative energy, meditating, exercising, and defining limits with energy vampires. Empaths need to regularly incorporate these forms of self-care into their lives. I'm also a big believer in personal rituals and meditations, such as the following one for grounding.

The Power of Grounding and Earthing

"Earthing" is a way of connecting to the earth to ground yourself. The earth's energy is medicine for stressed-out humans. Touching the earth lets you take her healing in through your feet and entire body. There is emerging science suggesting that Earthing is beneficial to our health—being in contact with the earth's electrons is believed to calm our nervous system. It's ideal to walk barefoot in nature, but it's also fine in a grassy backyard. Your feet are especially good at grounding stress because of the many reflexology and acupuncture points in the soles. These are activated by walking barefoot and by massaging them. Your feet are perfectly positioned to transmit the earth's healing to the rest of you. You can also lay your entire body on the earth for a fuller effect. I love resting on my back by the ocean, gazing at the sky.

But if being in nature is not an option for you, you can use the following visualization at home, at work, or even in a social situation. If you don't have a private space, you can always take a break and sit outside or simply go to the bathroom for a few minutes. (For years, the bathroom has been my refuge when I've needed to escape from a gathering to lower my stimulation level.) Practice this visualization to decompress and return to your center. I use it for at least five minutes daily and teach it to my patients. With this meditation and all the others in the book, you might want to read the directions into a tape recorder, and then when you're ready to meditate, you can simply play it back and relax into the meditation.

PROTECTION STRATEGY
Grounding and Earthing Visualization

Whenever you feel overloaded, anxious, or fearful, take some quiet time to lower your stimulation level. Being alone to recharge will help you decompress. Remember to turn off the computer and phone. Sit in a comfortable position and take a few deep breaths to relax your body. Feel the stillness and ease as tension begins to melt away. There is nothing to do and nothing to be. Just breathe and relax. When thoughts come, let them drift by like clouds in the sky. Do not attach to them. Focus only on slowly inhaling and then exhaling. Feel stress leaving your body as you connect to a sense of serenity.

In this tranquil inner space, visualize a large tree with a wide, strong trunk that extends down the center of your body, from head to toe. Take a few moments to feel its power and vibrant energy. Then visualize the tree's roots growing from the bottom of your feet and rooting down into the ground, making their way deeper and deeper, creating a comforting sense of solidity. Focus on these roots when you are anxious or afraid. Let the roots anchor you into Mother Earth, stabilizing you. Rooting yourself in this way provides an inner strength that will keep you centered and protected when life gets overwhelming. As you gently and slowly open your eyes, continue to feel the sensation of grounding. Come back to the outer world knowing that you can use this visualization to anchor yourself whenever you get thrown off balance. ◼

Grounding is an essential skill to keep you strong. *Focusing on your feet, not your fears or sense of overwhelm, is a quick way to center yourself.* Foot massage also works wonders to get you out of your head and into your body. Regularly practice this Earthing meditation, as well as others I'll be sharing, to reduce sensory overload.

THE BLESSING OF BEING AN EMPATH

As you begin this journey with me, remember that your presence, your sweetness, your tender appreciation for people and all of life are gifts, for you and others. Your intuition and your refined sensitivities are healing. I want you to appreciate yourself, your openness and your ability to feel. Realize how special and perfect you are. When you really see yourself, you can connect with the wholeness and depth within. Then you can enjoy your empathy—and that's the point. Not everyone will understand you, but that's okay. Search for kindred spirits who will, and you will understand them too. It's a beautiful feeling of connection. Later, I will discuss how to create empath support groups by using this book and its companion audio program, *Essential Tools for Empaths.* In the support group, you can read sections of the book or listen to the audio and then discuss how the information relates to your issues as empaths. It's amazingly freeing to give and receive such support.

———

We are in the midst of an evolution of human consciousness, and empaths are the path forgers. A sacred responsibility comes with our sensitivities, which demand more of us than simply retreating into isolation. It's vital we learn how to avoid feeling overwhelmed so that we can fully shine our power in the world. Empaths and all sensitive people are pioneers on the forefront of a new way of being for humankind.

You are part of Generation S, for Sensitivity—those who salute compassion and loving-kindness. You represent a vital opening for humanity to grow into a more heart-centered and intuitive awareness. You can model for others how to be sensitive and powerful.

I am passionate about helping you manage your sensitivities and use them for your personal well-being and the greater good. Just as I've learned to honor myself as an empath, which makes me feel incredibly whole, I hope you will honor your gifts too. I want the information in this book to empower you to be more yourself than you ever have been. To begin this journey, I offer you the following affirmation.

EMPATH AFFIRMATION

I vow to honor my sensitivities
and treat myself lovingly
as I explore what it means
to be an empath and embrace
my gifts. I will appreciate
myself every day.

Chapter 2

EMPATHS, EMOTIONS, AND HEALTH

How to Stop Absorbing Other People's Distress

An empath's body is different from other people's. We feel everything. Our bodies are porous so we absorb the positive and negative energies around us into our muscles, tissues, and organs. This can affect our health in many important ways. On the positive side, we're able to sense other people's vitality, happiness, and love within ourselves. This feels amazing and is such good medicine! However, we can also feel other people's physical discomfort, stress, and negative emotions, such as frustration, anger, and fear (even when they're unspoken). As empaths, we can get tired and sick when we're around toxic people, noise, violence, rushing, and yelling.

We can even manifest what I call "empathic illnesses," where we experience someone else's physical symptoms as if they were our own. As I child, when I'd get on the bus, my mood would suddenly change. I'd start feeling the anxiety or pain of the person beside me. Or I'd go into a large grocery store feeling perfectly fine yet leave exhausted and tense or with an ache or a pain I didn't have before. I had no idea then that I was being overwhelmed by dizzying aisles of food choices, noxious florescent lighting, and the long lines of people. What all this eventually told me about myself, and my patients, was that certain settings are more stressful for empaths and that other people's emotions and symptoms can get stuck in our bodies.

To survive as an empath, it's essential to learn both how to stop absorbing other people's emotions and pain and how to ground ourselves in overstimulating environments that are not empath friendly. I will teach you these skills in this chapter. Once you can apply the basics of self-protection, the world will be much easier to navigate, and your health and sense of wellness will improve.

THE LIMITATIONS OF TURNING TO MAINSTREAM MEDICINE

Conventional health care has some serious definciencies when it comes to helping sensitive people. Empaths are often misdiagnosed as hypochondriacs or neurotics, a frustrating way to be treated when you're vulnerable and in need, or they may be sent to a psychiatrist for a prescription for an antidepressant such as Prozac or anti-anxiety medications such as Valium or Xanax. Although these are often the standard biochemical treatments for depression and anxiety in conventional medicine, they are not what I recommend for empathic overload.

Additionally, in mainstream medicine, empaths may be diagnosed with Sensory Processing Disorder, a condition which is associated with an impaired ability to process sensory stimulation. Those with this diagnosis are considered to be "abnormally" sensitive to crowds, light, sound, and touch. I am very against physicians labeling high sensitivity as a sensory processing "disorder" instead of a gift with its own set of challenges. Medicine too often pathologizes anything "different" that it doesn't understand. Empaths have special traits that exist on the normal continuum of human experience. They exemplify the wonderful diversity of our species.

The problem with conventional medicine is that it lacks a paradigm that includes the body's subtle energy system. This concept has been central to many healing traditions for thousands of years cross-culturally, including traditional Chinese medicine. What is subtle energy? It is the vital life force that penetrates the body and extends inches to feet around it. Think of the halo in sacred art, the beautiful white light that comes off the top of the head; that's an example of the energy body. Unlike traditional Chinese medical practitioners, who work with their patients' subtle energy, known as chi, conventional medical practitioners do not share this reference point when diagnosing and treating patients—a limitation that is crucial for you to grasp. My mission is to re-educate healthcare practitioners about the proper treatment of empaths, who are incredibly energy sensitive, so that we can get the care and understanding we deserve.

In my psychotherapy practice, I combine my conventional medical skills with energy medicine, intuition, and spirituality. (In my audio program *Becoming an Intuitive Healer*, I help to train healthcare practitioners and those in the service professions to develop these skills too.) When patients consult with me, I listen with my intellect, but I also listen with my intuition and empathic abilities. This extra information saves me enormous time in getting to know them. To empower my empath patients, I teach them to tune into their inner voice and to set boundaries with draining people, so that their sensitivities can be a source of strength, love, and vitality rather than "dis-ease."

OPTIMIZING YOUR HEALTH: ARE YOU A PHYSICAL OR EMOTIONAL EMPATH?

It is vital for empaths to take a conscious approach to their health. The first step to optimizing your energy level is to identify whether you're a physical or an emotional empath—or even both. Knowing this will help you understand how your sensitivities function so that you can build stamina and protect yourself from getting depleted.

Physical empaths feel other people's symptoms in their own bodies. For instance, a friend complains of a stomachache, and suddenly an empath's stomach starts hurting too. Or a coworker has a migraine, and an empath's head starts throbbing too. The upside of being a physical empath is that they can absorb other people's experience of well-being. One of my patients told me that when she takes a yoga class, her empath spouse feels the relaxation in his body as well even though he's in another part of town. He receives the benefits of her yoga practice as well!

Emotional empaths mainly pick up other people's emotions. They can sit beside a depressed person while watching a comedy and walk out of the movie theater feeling depressed. How? The other person's energy field overlaps with the empath's field during the film. The nearer an empath is to someone, the more they will be influenced by the person's emotions and symptoms. The problem is that emotional empaths often have no clue which emotions belong to them and which belong to someone else. They may get thrown off by others' feelings without realizing it or knowing how to re-center themselves. As one patient told me, "It takes me a full day to recuperate from being around an extremely negative or angry person."

But there are solutions. A big aha! moment for another patient, Terry, was realizing that she'd been absorbing her mother's anxiety since childhood. Empaths have big hearts and often unconsciously take on their loved one's emotions. Once Terry became aware of this dynamic, however, I could teach her to set boundaries. I had her visualize cutting an energetic cord between her mother's anxiety and herself. This allowed Terry to maintain a healthy boundary while still remaining a caring daughter to her mother.

Both physical and emotional empaths make good medical intuitives when their abilities are trained. They can diagnose disease in others by empathically sensing other people's symptoms. To protect their own health, however, they must also become skilled at releasing what they pick up.

The goal for all empaths is to lead more comfortable lives by learning how to stop soaking up negative energy. We may instinctively want to take away another's pain, but that's not healthy for us. I've learned to be present for my patients and workshop participants without shouldering their discomfort. Since I frequently give seminars and speak in front of hundreds of people at a time, it's essential that I ground and protect myself. This allows me to do the teaching I love and not get worn out by excessive stimulation. Throughout this book, I'll continue to share effective tools that I use in my own life to be a balanced empath.

Physical and Emotional Empath Self-Assessments

To stay in good health, it's important to determine whether you're a physical or an emotional empath. Like me, you might even be both. Knowing more about which type of empath you are will allow you to take clear steps toward self-care. Here are two self-assessments to determine what type of empath you are.

~~~~~~~~~~~~~~~~~~~~~~~~~~~~~~

SELF-ASSESSMENT Am I a Physical or Emotional Empath?

AM I A PHYSICAL EMPATH?

Ask yourself the following questions:

- Have I ever sat next to someone in pain and started to feel pain too?
- Do I get physically ill in crowds?
- Have I been called a hypochondriac but know my symptoms are real?
- Do I react to other people's stress by developing a physical symptom in my own body?
- Do I get energized by some people and depleted by others?
- Do I frequently go to doctors without getting treatments that help?
- Am I chronically fatigued, or do I have mysterious and unexplained ailments?
- Do I often feel exhausted by crowds, preferring to stay home?
- Is my body sensitive to sugar, alcohol, and processed foods?

AM I AN EMOTIONAL EMPATH?

Ask yourself the following questions:

- Do I pick up other people's emotions, such as anxiety, anger, or frustration?

- Do I get an emotional hangover after an argument or a conflict?

- Do I feel depressed or anxious in crowds?

- Do I want to fix people and take away their stress?

- Can I intuit other people's feelings, even when they are unexpressed?

- Is it hard to distinguish other people's emotions from my own?

- Do I care so much about others that I neglect my own needs?

- Do I overeat to cope with difficult people or emotional stress?

- Do I experience mood swings from sugar, carbohydrates, or other specific foods?

Here's how to interpret the self-assessments:

- One to two yeses in a category indicate that you're partially that type of empath.

- Three to four yeses indicate that you are moderately that type of empath.

- Five or more yeses indicate that you're definitely that type of empath.

~~~~~~~~~~~~~~~~~~

Discovering that you are a physical or emotional empath—or both—is important knowledge about yourself and how to cope with the world. You are not crazy or a hypochondriac. You are a sensitive person with a gift that you must develop and successfully manage.

EMPATHIC ILLNESSES

I have coined the term "empathic illness" to mean illnesses in which someone manifests symptoms that are not their own. Yes, it's possible to catch these from other people! Such symptoms feel like they're yours, but they are not—a confusing predicament. For instance, one of my patients, Alicia, actually felt her asthmatic sister's shortness of breath in her own body, even though she didn't have the condition. Another patient, Brian, was so connected to his wife that his hand would hurt in sympathy with flare-ups in her arthritis. Some illnesses are totally empathic.

More often, though, picking up other people's "dis-ease" will aggravate symptoms an empath already has. In severe cases, empathic illnesses can leave people chronically ill, housebound, and paralyzed by social anxiety. Empaths are prone to social anxiety because they're overwhelmed by the multiple spoken and unspoken signals people give off in groups; empaths are also sensitive to rejection. These individuals become so exhausted and burned out from feeling the world's stress that they can't function. Again, because conventional medicine does not believe in the existence of the body's subtle energy system, most doctors have no context for understanding what's going on with empaths or how to relieve their suffering.

Many patients come to me with these common empathic-related illnesses:

- adrenal fatigue
- autoimmune diseases, such as Hashimoto's thyroiditis and inflammatory bowel disease
- agoraphobia (the fear of going outside)
- phobias (for example, of crowds, driving, or large stadium events)

- chronic depression
- chronic fatigue
- fibromyalgia
- pain
- panic attacks and social anxiety

Over twenty years ago, when I first started treating empaths in my psychotherapy practice, I didn't know how to adequately help them with their symptoms. I was just learning to cope with being an empath myself. However, when I took a careful history, I found that most of these patients were in close contact with a loved one or coworker in distress and were unknowingly absorbing that person's emotions and symptoms. I could relate because I did this too! Other empaths responded strongly to changes in the natural world. I had one patient whose back pain grew worse during thunderstorms. Some experienced seasonal affective disorder (SAD), a depression that occurs in the winter, when days are shorter and darker. Also, many empaths felt more restless and anxious on a full moon, while calm on a new moon.

THE PEOPLE WHO ARE SENSITIVE IN LIFE MAY SUFFER MUCH MORE THAN THOSE WHO ARE INSENSITIVE, BUT IF THEY UNDERSTAND AND GO BEYOND THEIR SUFFERING, THEY WILL DISCOVER EXTRAORDINARY THINGS.

Jiddu Krishnamurti

Realizing the exquisite sensitivities of empaths and their inability to modulate them has significantly changed how I treat these patients. My job has become about teaching them grounding techniques and how to set healthy boundaries to protect themselves. The correct treatment for empathic illnesses is to train these sensitive people to stop absorbing the energy and stress of others, rather than medicating their symptoms. Then they can stop fighting exhaustion and overwhelm and experience vibrant health.

EMPATHS AND MEDICATION

Many physicians go straight to antidepressants and antianxiety medications when treating empaths, but I try not to use them initially with such sensitive souls. Sometimes my patients just need to be kinder to themselves and make small adjustments to ease their lives. For instance, Jane came to me with intense anxiety when she drove on the Los Angeles freeways. The multiple lanes of cars and the huge trucks whizzing by in both directions overwhelmed her and made her lightheaded. Many empaths, including myself, have this aversion to freeways. The high-speed traffic and upset drivers are just too much for some of us to process. I have not driven on the freeways for years!

Although Jane had practiced deep breathing exercises before getting into the car and took shorter freeway trips to get used to driving, these strategies were not sufficient. Her physician suggested anti-anxiety meds, but she wasn't comfortable taking them. I presented Jane with a simple alternative. Instead of continuing to make herself crazy trying to "get over" her driving anxiety, she could give herself permission to avoid freeways when possible and take some wonderful side streets throughout the city—the way I do. Jane felt tremendous relief with this solution. She simply allowed for more travel time. I also urged her to stop pressuring herself to "be like other people," a mistake many sensitive people make. Empaths often have special needs that must be respected, and these needs are okay. We're not failing or copping out by finding ways to be kind to ourselves. The softer and easier solution to a problem can be a merciful way to resolve anxiety, without having to turn to medication.

However, once some empaths have been chronically depleted by trauma or stress, they may well require medication for depression and anxiety to rebalance their biochemistry. I prescribe such medication mainly for the short term. I find it interesting that many empaths require a much lower dose than other people do to get a positive effect. For instance, a sliver of an antidepressant can work wonders for my highly sensitive patients. A mainstream physician might write this off as a placebo response, but I disagree. Empaths are just more sensitive to everything, including medication. We often can't tolerate the usual doses that conventional medicine deems effective. If you're an empath who needs medication, I suggest working with an integrative healthcare practitioner who understands subtle energy and can find the best dosage for your body.

I'm also fascinated by new research on how pain medications can inhibit empathy. Ohio State University researchers recently found that when participants who took Tylenol (acetaminophen) learned about the mishaps of others, they experienced less dismay than those who didn't take the drug.[1] Knowing that Tylenol decreases empathy is important since fifty-two million Americans take a substance containing it every week!

EMPATHS AND ADRENAL FATIGUE

Adrenal fatigue is a common health issue for empaths. Some of my patients come in with this syndrome, which is a collection of symptoms including exhaustion, body aches and pains, anxiety, trouble thinking clearly, and insomnia. What is the cause? One theory is that the adrenal glands can't keep up with incoming stress, so hormones such as cortisol, which normally are energizing, become depleted. Because empaths also absorb other people's symptoms, this adds to their stress levels and leaves them vulnerable to adrenal fatigue.

What follows are some solutions for treating adrenal fatigue. Using them can help turn around symptoms and restore energy. But remember, these solutions aren't a one-time fix. Overcoming adrenal fatigue requires some basic lifestyle and diet changes so that empaths can effectively manage their energy over the long term. Along with the following tips, I will discuss a range of strategies throughout this book.

PROTECTION STRATEGY
Tips to Relieve Adrenal Fatigue

- **Eat a whole-food diet.** Avoid processed and junk foods, gluten, sugar, and white flour. (You'll learn more in chapter 3.)

- **Add Himalayan Red Salt to your diet.** Eliminate low-quality salts. (Always check with your physician about your salt intake if your blood pressure is high.)

- **Exercise.** Practice gentle exercise and stretching to build up stamina and energy.

- **Meditate.** Meditation increases endorphins, which are natural painkillers, and reduces stress hormones.

- **Get a blood test to measure your cortisol level.** If your cortisol level is low, consider temporary natural cortisol replacement per your physician's recommendation.

- **Rest a lot.** Sleep is restorative and healing.

- **Take B vitamins daily.**

- **Take 2,000 to 5,000 mg of vitamin C daily in the acute phase.**

- **Consider IV vitamin C drips** (10,000 to 25,000 mg). This will increase your energy and immunity, and to support adrenal health. Holistic physicians often offer this treatment. I do this when I'm coming down with a cold to strengthen my immune system.

- **Eliminate the energy vampires in your life.** Try to rid yourself of toxic people or at least set clear limits and boundaries so they don't sap you. (More about this in chapter 5.) ■

In addition, be kind to yourself and stay positive. Focus on wellness, not illness. Do not beat yourself up with negative thoughts such as, "I will never feel better" or "I am weak and sick." No matter what's happening in your life, you always have control of your attitude. To relieve adrenal fatigue, you can reduce inner stress by showing self-compassion.

EMPATHS AND EXERCISE

Regular exercise is lifesaving for empaths because it physically expels tension and negative energy. A sedentary lifestyle causes your energy flow to stagnate, allowing all kinds of toxins to accumulate. When you feel stress building, take a walk, go to the gym or a yoga class, or do some stretching. Vigorous exercise is excellent at purifying our system, though gentle exercise can be effective too. Movement keeps us flexible so our muscles don't contract and hold in negativity. In this way, exercise turns back the clock, helping us to stay younger and more vital.

SELF-PROTECTION FOR EMPATHS: 14 STRATEGIES TO COMBAT TOXIC ENERGY

My patients frequently ask, "How can I tell if my emotions or symptoms are mine or someone else's? And if they're not mine, how do I let them go?" The answers are key to becoming a happy and energized person.

Here are some basic strategies to practice if you think you're absorbing the stress or symptoms of others and need to release the negative energy. I use these strategies in my life and teach them to my patients and workshop participants. Experiment to see which ones work best for you.

Strategy 1. Ask yourself, "Is this symptom or emotion mine or someone else's?"

A tip-off that you're absorbing someone's energy is to notice when you experience a sudden change of mood or physical state around a person. If you didn't feel anxious, depressed, exhausted, or sick before, most likely the discomfort you're feeling now is at least partially coming from someone else. If your discomfort dissipates when you're not near this person, it is probably not yours!

Sometimes, though, the emotion or symptom may belong to both another person and you. Feelings are catching, especially if they relate to a hot-button issue for you. For instance, if you have unresolved anger at your father, you'll soak up other people's anger at their fathers. Or if you fear chronic illness, you will be susceptible to absorbing the symptoms of chronic illnesses that others have. Empaths are more prone to take on the emotional or physical pain that they haven't worked out in themselves. The more you heal issues that trigger you, the less likely you will be to absorb such symptoms from others. You might still sense them, but they won't impact you as deeply or drain you.

Strategy 2. Breathe and repeat this mantra

When negativity strikes, immediately focus on your breath for a few minutes. Slowly and deeply inhale and exhale to expel the uncomfortable energy. Breathing circulates negativity out of your body. Holding the breath and breathing shallowly keep negativity stuck inside you. As you breathe deeply, I also suggest repeating this mantra aloud, three times, in a tone that conveys you mean what you're saying:

Return to sender. Return to sender. Return to sender.

The power of your voice can command the discomfort out of your body, while your breath is the vehicle that transports the discomfort back to the universe.

Also, while saying this mantra, you can focus on breathing toxic energy out of your lumbar spine, which is your lower back. The spaces between the lumbar vertebrae act as channels for eliminating symptoms you might have picked up. Visualize the discomfort exiting through these spaces in your spine. Declare, "I release you," as the unhealthy energy leaves your body and blends with the giant energy matrix of life.

Strategy 3. Step away from what's disturbing you

Move at least twenty feet from the suspected source of discomfort. See if you feel relief. Don't worry about offending strangers. Whether you're in a doctor's office, movie theater, or other public places, don't hesitate to change seats. If you're sitting next to a noisy group in a restaurant, you don't have to stay there and feel uncomfortable. Feel free to move to a more peaceful table. These are strategies I use to take care of myself. It's fine to lovingly say "no" to certain energies. Giving yourself permission to move is an act of self-care.

This is what an empath friend told me he did at a noisy graduation party. "I had to leave for a while because the noise and crowd were too intense. Dinner hadn't yet been served, but my ears were ringing. I was on edge. So I sat in my car for an hour with my book of poetry while the group at the celebration enjoyed dinner and dancing. I told my friends that I needed to take a break and rest, which they understood. In the end, they had fun at the party, and I had some quiet time to center myself before I returned."

Empaths often find themselves in overwhelming social situations. When that happens to you, be sure to take breaks to replenish yourself. Then, if you want to return to the gathering, you will be in a more serene place.

Strategy 4. Limit physical contact; hugs are a choice

Energy is transferred through the eyes and touch. If you're uncomfortable with someone, limit eye contact and touch, including hugs and holding hands. Though hugging a loved one in distress often benefits you both, if you are wary of taking on their stress, make the hug short. You can keep sending them love from a distance.

It's with respect that many healers, who understand energy, ask people they first meet, "Is it okay to hug you?" You can ask permission too. It's also fine to nicely say "no" to a hug request. I sometimes tell people "I don't hug" if I'm not prepared to share energy with them. Until you're fully at ease with someone, you might also choose to give a "half hug"—the kind where you pat a person on the back. When you feel safer in the relationship, you can transition to a complete hug and feel good about it. Remember that you always have a choice about the kind of physical contact you want to participate in.

Strategy 5. Detox in water

A quick way to dissolve stress and empathic pains is to immerse yourself in water. Empaths love water! Epsom salt baths are divine, providing magnesium, which is calming. My bath is a sanctuary after a busy day. Being in water washes away everything from bus exhaust, to long hours of air travel, to pesky symptoms I might have picked up from others. You might want to add a little lavender essential oil to your bath, which is most calming after a long day. The perfect getaway for an empath is soaking in natural mineral springs, which purify all that ails us.

Strategy 6. Set limits and boundaries

There's no way around it: to survive and thrive, we need to set limits with people. If someone is draining, don't be a door-mat. Control how much time you spend listening to the person. *"No" is a complete sentence.* It's okay to tell someone what your needs and preferences are: for example, "I'm sorry, but I'm not up for going to a party tonight," or "Let's discuss this when you're calmer because I can't tolerate yelling," or "I need to meditate and be quiet right now," or "I can't talk for more than a few minutes unless you want to discuss solutions." Sometimes changing communication patterns with those who know us is a retraining process, but being consistent with kind but firm limits will protect you from energy vampires.

Strategy 7. Visualize cutting a cord between you and the other person

If you feel you are too connected with someone's unpleasant physical or emotional state, visualize a cord of light extending from your belly to theirs, and then lovingly set the intention to cut that cord. You're not severing the connection with the person entirely—only with the unwelcome energy they carry. Now visualize taking a pair of scissors and cutting the cord between you and the unwelcome energy in that person. This is the technique my patient Terry, whom I mentioned earlier, used to separate herself from her mother's anxiety while main-taining a loving bond with her.

Strategy 8. Plan alone time to regroup

Empaths need alone time to reconnect with their power. If you've picked up unwanted energy, be sure to plan some alone time to center yourself. For a few minutes or more, quiet everything.

No noise, bright lights, phone calls, texts, emails, Internet, television, or conversations. It's important to feel your own energy without anyone else around. You are being your own best friend, which is a way to nurture yourself. Decreasing external stimulation also makes it easier to clear negativity. To counter any stress I've taken on from others, I get very quiet and go inward to connect with my own energy and heart. When I'm in my center, others people's discomfort doesn't cling to me.

> SOMETIMES I NEED
> TO GO OFF ON MY
> OWN. I'M NOT SAD.
> I'M NOT ANGRY.
> I'M JUST RECHARGING
> MY BATTERIES.
> **Kristen Butler**

Strategy 9. Spend time in nature and practice Earthing

Empaths love nature and feel at ease there. Being in a fresh, clean, green environment, as well as near water, clears negativity. The earth emanates healing. Try lying down in a meadow and allowing your entire body to soak up its energy. This feels sublime! As I've already noted, Earthing means going barefoot and feeling the earth's power through your feet. To shed other people's energy, simply feel the grass on your bare toes, or walk in sand or soil. Sense the nurturing medicine of the earth coming through your feet to ground you. It's a beautiful experience. I love being barefoot—in fact, I've never really liked wearing shoes, unless it's cold or I'm not home.

I feel strongly about the importance of taking personal retreat time away from the world at least once a year. This is a planned break to decompress in nature or a calming place where you can recalibrate your system. I offer a yearly weekend retreat for sensitive people at Esalen Institute by the gorgeous redwoods and ocean in Big Sur, California. It's a time for participants to slow down, tune in to their intuition, and connect more deeply to their spirit. I also take a few personal retreats on my own each year in nature, to get off the grid and restore myself.

Strategy 10. Get plenty of sleep and take power naps

Sleep is a healing balm for an empath's body and soul. It calms the nervous system. Empaths are more vulnerable to absorbing stress and symptoms when they are tired. That's why it's crucial to get enough sleep. As a self-care rule, honor the sleep time you need to replenish yourself every night. If you're feeling especially stressed, plan on getting extra sleep, and take short power naps during the day if you can. Sleep heals like nothing else can. To feel at my best, I need eight hours of sleep a night.

A calm, peaceful period before sleeping, when you reflect on the day or meditate, is important. No Internet, social media, paying bills, intense conversations, newscasts, or violent TV (some people believe the bedroom is just for rest, sleep, and sex, and don't allow televisions there). A soothing environment reduces your stimulation level so you can sleep better and travel to different realms in your dreams. Easing into sleep and not rushing your way there is especially healthy for empaths. Waking up slowly is also ideal, rather than bolting out of bed. Allow yourself to remember your dreams in the morning. Let your bed be your healing temple. One empath joked with me, "I like my bed more than I like most people." I can relate. I love my sleep and dreamtime too. If I don't get enough of either, my system feels off, and I'm more likely to absorb other people's stress.

Strategy 11. Take breaks from being online

Empaths need regular timeouts from technology, which inundates us with too much information. Online media—such as Facebook, Instagram, and news feeds with upsetting information—trigger our emotions and can impair our ability to fall asleep. It's easy to pick up energy from the virtual world, so make sure you spend time in nature, meditating, or participating in other offline activities that restore you. A technology fast every once in a while will also do wonders for your sense of well-being.

Strategy 12. Clearing tips for traveling

Whether for business or pleasure, the stress of traveling can expose us to toxic energy that may not normally enter our everyday life. We're dealing with airports, cramped planes or trains, hotels, and new people. The following suggestions are ways that we can travel more comfortably and not get overwhelmed by the crowds and close quarters.

How to Stay Centered in Airports and on Planes

Airports can be especially difficult for empaths. Because airports are noisy, crowded, rushed, and full of all kinds of stressful energies swirling around, they can be particularly overwhelming for empaths. To deal with the chaos, stay focused within your personal energy bubble. Instead of concentrating on the harried people around you, concentrate on your heart energy to self-soothe. When waiting for a plane, I'll often put my purse and papers on the seat beside me to create a circle of personal space. If someone needs to sit there and I'm uneasy with the person's energy, I'll pick up my things and move. No excuses necessary. I do this with love, not anger.

Being on a plane can also induce sensory overload. The density of people in such a confined space can provoke anxiety in empaths because there is no escape. Here are some tips to make your flight easier:

- Check your luggage so you don't have to fight for overhead bins.

- Choose an aisle seat so you get out easily and take refuge in the bathroom if necessary.

- To avoid the crowd boarding the plane, wait until the other passengers have boarded and then casually walk on to take your seat.

- Bring clothes to keep you warm since the air-conditioning can be chilly.

- Bring water to stay hydrated.

- Try wearing an air purifier around your neck, which generates negative ions to purify the stale, recirculated air on the plane.

- Use earbuds to eliminate unwanted noise and enjoy listening to music or an uplifting audiobook instead.

- Avoid draining conversations with others. Strangers tend to tell their life stories to empaths. Unless you are drawn to talk to someone, create a cone of silence around yourself that communicates "I'm not available."

- Center yourself by meditating.

- During any turbulence, stay grounded by placing your attention on your feet rather than your fear.

Remember that your feet contain many powerful reflexology points and acupuncture meridians that can center you, even when you're thirty thousand feet in the air. Simply concentrating on your feet will divert your anxiety from your head to your feet, which will naturally release the anxious energy.

How to Stay Centered in Hotel Rooms

To clear the energy left behind by previous guests in hotel rooms, I suggest spraying rose water or lavender essential oil (or both) to purify the space. I also practice the Three-Minute Heart Meditation (described below) to remove negative energy. For years, I used to change hotel rooms frequently to find the one with the best energy, but then one day my Daoist teacher told me that it's more empowering to stick with the room I'm given and to practice clearing the energy myself.

When traveling, take care to stay hydrated and to eat regular protein meals for grounding. As empaths, we can get into trouble when we skip meals, binge on sugar, or don't get enough rest—choices that weaken our defenses and set us up to absorb unwanted energies. If you're taking on stress from others, practice breathing it out. If you start feeling overstimulated or drained, find a place to meditate and center yourself. With all these options, you can feel more at ease and have more fun on your travel adventures. Enjoy the new cultures and terrain, and revel in the benefits of being an empath!

Strategy 13. Practice the Three-Minute Heart Meditation

To counter emotional or physical distress, respond quickly by removing yourself from the immediate toxic situation to meditate for as little as three minutes. You can do this at home, at work, on a park bench, or in a bathroom at parties.

PROTECTION STRATEGY
The Three-Minute Heart Meditation

Close your eyes. Take a few deep breaths and relax. Then place your palm over your heart chakra, in the middle of your chest. Focus on a beautiful image you love, such as a sunset, a rose, the ocean, a child's face. Feel the love building in your heart and body. Let this loving feeling soothe you. Toxic energy leaves your body as you become purified with love. For just three minutes, meditate on the loving-kindness in your heart and feeling that energy clear stress. You might want to nurture yourself with three-minute bursts of this meditation throughout your day.

You can send this loving-kindness to specific areas of your body too. My most vulnerable point is my gut. If I sense that I've taken on someone else's symptom, I place my hand over my belly and send it loving-kindness. This dissolves my discomfort. What is your most sensitive point? Is it your neck? Do you get bladder infections? Headaches? Send these areas loving-kindness to clear away toxic energy so it doesn't lodge there.

Sometimes it's easier to meditate on the well-being of someone else (which opens your heart too) rather than yourself. Do this if you're having a hard time meditating on yourself. ∎

Come back to your heart often as it is the seat of unconditional love. When you're under stress, put your hand on your heart, and feel the sensations of warmth, opening, and love. You're protected, you're loved, and you're safe.

Strategy 14. Be fully present in your body

Empaths are most protected when we are fully present in our body. Forge a loving relationship with the body instead of fearing it, loathing it, or existing as a disembodied head. Empaths need to be in their bodies to ward off unwanted energies. Your body is the temple that houses your spirit. See it as a friend rather than an enemy. The following meditation will help you make a commitment to fully inhabit your body so that you can be more present and joyous.

PROTECTION STRATEGY
Meditation for Loving Your Empath Body

Find time for solitude in a beautiful space. Don't force the mind to quiet but rather shift channels. Take a few deep breaths. Feel each inhalation and exhalation. Slow yourself down so that you can be more aware of your body. Let any negative thoughts float by while you return to your breath, the sacred prana. Feel its motion bring you into your deeper self. Settle your energy within the bounds of your body, cells, and organs.

Become aware of your toes. Wiggle them and note the beautiful feeling of awakening the feet. Next, bring your awareness to your ankles. As you continue breathing, move your focus up your legs to your knees. Then continue to bring your attention up to your strong thighs, and note how grounding they feel. Inwardly thank them for holding you up. Then bring your awareness to your genitals and pelvic area. Many women experience clenching here. You might want to inwardly say, "I recognize you. I'm not turning my back on you anymore. I'm going to learn about you and love you. You are part of me."

Move your awareness now to your belly. Are you holding any tension, burning, or other discomfort there? This is the chakra where we process emotions. Soothe and heal this area by bringing loving awareness to your belly. Focus on your chest now, where your heart chakra resides, the center for unconditional love. Make it your friend so you can be loving to yourself. Feel a shower of positive energy coursing through your heart. Return here often to feel the nurturing energy. Now, expand this awareness to your shoulders, arms, wrists, and beautiful hands. Feel and move each finger. These are all an extension of the heart chakra.

Next, bring your attention to your neck. The communication chakra resides in the throat area. Notice if you feel any tension here that would stop you from expressing yourself. Send love to this area.

Now, bring your awareness to your head, feeling your beautiful face, your ears, mouth, eyes, nose, and third eye, which resides between your eyebrows. This is the center for intuition. You might see swirling purple colors in your mind's eye as you tune in. Finally, bring your attention to the top of your head. This is the crown chakra, the center for white light, your connection to Spirit. Feel the inspiration that emanates from here.

When you are ready to conclude this meditation, inwardly say "thank you" for the experience of feeling present in your body. Affirm to yourself, "I am ready to come into my full power as an embodied empath." Take a few deep breaths. Then slowly and gently open your eyes. Return fully to your environment, more aware of your body than ever. ■

You can enlist these fourteen strategies in a wide variety of situations. Use them often, and then stress or pain won't build up in your body. As you continue to practice them, you'll feel the great benefits of protecting your sensitivities. Practice is the secret to success. These strategies will strengthen your health so you can feel more energized. When you notice that you're picking up other people's pain or emotions, don't panic. This happens. As much as you work to clear negativity, outside energy will sneak in, but with the strategies I've shared here, you can initiate self-care quickly in whatever stressful situation you find yourself in.

When it comes to our health, the mind-body connection is powerful. Bear in mind that our thoughts make a profound difference. Negative thoughts increase the flow of stress hormones, which accelerate aging, decrease immunity, and increase anxiety, blood pressure, and heart disease. On the other hand, positive thoughts boost the flow of endorphins, the body's natural painkillers and feel-good hormones, promoting health and calmness. So, cultivate positive self-talk. Remember to show yourself compassion, particularly when you're ill, stressed, or emotionally distraught. Affirm to yourself daily, "I deserve to be happy and healthy," and "There is always hope." Replacing negative thoughts with positive ones will enhance your well-being.

Do your best to relax and flow through all your experiences, whether uplifting or difficult and all those in-between. When we tighten up, it only makes pain worse. I tell my patients, "If you're in hell, you might as well relax because relaxing will at least decrease your suffering." And when you are in heaven—and you will be more and more—savor every minute of it with your empath self.

EMPATH AFFIRMATION

I am strong. I am loving.
I am positive. I have the power
to clear all negativity and stress
from my body. I embrace my
physical, emotional, and
spiritual wellness.

Chapter 3

EMPATHS AND ADDICTION

From Alcohol to Overeating

Empaths commonly self-medicate the discomfort of being overstimulated by turning to alcohol, drugs, sex, food, gambling, shopping, or other addictions. Why are empaths so susceptible to these behaviors? We can get overwhelmed by our extreme sensitivity and "feel too much," including our own and another's pain. Since we may not know how to manage this sensory overload, we numb ourselves to shut off our thoughts and feelings, to diminish the empathy we experience—though not everyone is aware of this motivation.

Since research has shown that painkillers such as Tylenol can decrease empathy, perhaps this is a subconscious draw for empaths to abuse them. Many of the patients I've treated who were in recovery from addictions have been empaths. This may help explain why sensitive people reach for painkillers, including alcohol, over-the-counter drugs, and prescription medications.

In my workshops and private practice, empaths who have struggled with addictions have needed to learn ways to center and protect themselves instead of self-medicating in this unhealthy way. One woman said to me, "For years I used alcohol to bury my feelings. I love rodeos but couldn't go to one without drinking. Being around crowds felt painful. Once I learned to protect myself, I could feel safe and have fun without drinking." Another man drank heavily when he traveled, but once he learned to protect himself, he realized, "I don't have to let everyone's energy wear at me and drink at an airport bar just to cope." Although some components of addiction are genetic and environmental (such as being raised by alcoholic parents), being an empath can play a significant role.

We pay a high price for coping with our sensitivities through addictions. They exhaust our body, mind, and spirit, creating illness, depression, and more anxiety as we try to manage an overstimulating world. At best, addictions only provide short-term relief from sensory overload, but in the long term, they stop working and worsen the feeling of being overwhelmed. In Native American tradition, it's believed that alcoholics and addicts leave themselves vulnerable to being possessed by negative forces because the substances keep them from being in touch with their spirits and bodies, making it easy for negativity to take hold. That's the last thing any of us wants to have happen!

In this chapter, I'll provide you with healthy alternatives to addictions. These require developing a mindful awareness of your triggers and a readiness to use the strategies I discuss, so you don't impulsively act out when you're stressed. Whether you periodically or regularly engage in addictive behaviors, your goal is to grow larger than your small, scared, addicted self and become a more empowered highly sensitive person.

ALTERNATIVES TO SELF-MEDICATING: STRATEGIES AND SOLUTIONS

Empaths need alternatives to self-medicating. A Twelve-Step Program is an important resource that supports people in staying clean and sober. For nearly three decades, I have been a member of Twelve-Step Programs, which have influenced my personal coping skills as an empath along with my teachings. In my first book, *Second Sight*, I describe how, as a teenage empath, I had premonitions that scared me and how I was overwhelmed by absorbing the energy of others. To shut off my sensitivities, I got heavily involved with drugs and alcohol. I was an introverted empath. So I used substances to become less anxious and more social with my friends and at parties, which decreased my feelings of not fitting in. At the time, I had no other skills for managing my overwhelming empathic abilities, intuition, and insecurities, so I reached for something external to shut them off. I had no idea what was happening to me, which is true of many empaths. With the buffer of drugs and alcohol, I could finally be in crowds with my friends without taking on other people's energies. It was a relief: I felt normal.

Of course, substances were not the answer. Fortunately, at those times in my life when I was on a destructive path and didn't know how to help myself, divine guidance mercifully intervened. After the harrowing car accident I described in chapter 1, my parents were afraid for my life and forced me to see a psychiatrist. He taught me the importance of integrating all facets of myself—intellectual, emotional, physical, empathic, intuitive, and spiritual. And so my healing journey as an empath began. A basic part of this learning has taken place in Twelve-Step Programs.

Self-Evaluation and Twelve-Step Programs

Though not all alcoholics or addicts absorb other people's energy, I've observed that many do. Unfortunately, many empaths remain undiagnosed and don't realize how overstimulation and high sensitivity fuel their addictive behaviors. It's therefore crucial to understand whether you're coping with your sensitivities by engaging in addictions. How do you know? Ask yourself the following questions:

- Have I ever thought, "Life would be so much better if I didn't overeat? Or drink? "

- Have I ever tried to stop overeating or using substances for a month but could only last a few days, despite my best intentions?

- Am I self-medicating to ease social anxiety or the stress I take on from the world?

If you suspect you are using alcohol, drugs, food, or other addictive behaviors to manage the sensory overload of being an empath, take some time to reflect on how you cope by evaluating the following statements.

~~~~~~

SELF-ASSESSMENT **I turn to substances or other addictions when . . .**

- I am overwhelmed by emotions, whether mine or another's.

- I am in emotional pain and feel frustrated, anxious, or depressed.

- My feelings are hurt.

- I feel uncomfortable in my own skin.

- I can't sleep.

- I feel emotionally unsafe in a situation.

- I feel criticized, blamed, or rejected.

- I feel shy, anxious, or don't fit in socially.

- I'm isolating at home, and I need confidence to go out in public.

- I'm tired and need an energy boost.

- I feel drained by energy vampires.

- I want to escape and shut out the world.

Here's how to interpret this self-assessment:

- Answering yes to even one statement indicates that you sometimes turn to an addiction to cope with your sensitivities.

- Answering yes to two to five of the statements indicates you are moderately relying on an addiction to self-medicate feelings of sensory overload.

- Answering yes to six or more of the statements indicates you are largely coping with your sensitivities by engaging in addictive behavior.

Self-awareness is liberating. No shame and no blame. By becoming aware of your addictive tendencies, you're gaining an understanding of how you cope with your empathic sensitivities. Now you can more productively deal with it. If you discover that you are using addictions to manage the sensory overload of being an empath, there are actions you can take to heal yourself.

First, it's necessary to identify your addiction. Honestly assess how much you drink or use other substances weekly. How often do you overeat to cope with feeling overwhelmed? Do you turn to other addictions—such as sex, love, gambling, shopping, work, video games, or the Internet—to lower your anxiety level or shut off your sensitivities? Be compassionate with yourself. See if you find a pattern of self-medicating your feelings. Self-medicating even once a week or once a month indicates that you may have an issue with addiction.

Second, it's crucial to realize that *nothing* on the outside—no substance, person, job, or amount of money—can ultimately make you feel comfortable with yourself and your sensitivities. Happiness is an inside job. You must learn to know, love, and accept yourself, a life-long process of discovery. The more you run from your sensitivities, the more uncomfortable you will be. As Buddha taught, there is no external refuge. Being in a Twelve-Step Program has been invaluable in reinforcing the power of this truth over and over again in my life.

Third, in an ongoing plan to address your addiction, you might want to consider attending Twelve-Step meetings such as Alcoholics Anonymous (AA), Narcotics Anonymous (NA), or Overeaters Anonymous (OA). Gamblers Anonymous (GA) and Debtors Anonymous (DA) will help with financial issues. Some great relationship-oriented Twelve-Step Programs include Al-Anon (for relatives and friends of alcoholics), Co-Dependents Anonymous (CoDA), and Sex and Love Addicts Anonymous (SLAA). These meetings will support your having healthy relationships, and they will also teach you how to set clear boundaries with people, which is especially critical for empaths.

All of these programs are spiritually oriented and use the Twelve-Step model to overcome addictions. I urge you to give them a try. See if you can relate to other people's stories while learning positive skills for managing your empathic abilities in a stressful world. Then you won't have to drink, use, overeat, or act out sexually to numb your sensitivities.

FINDING SOLACE IN SPIRIT

In Twelve-Step Programs, spirituality is vital for recovering addicts to reclaim their power as they plug into the energy of love. We can wear ourselves out by people pleasing, being hypervigilant about sensing danger, or absorbing stress from others without a defense. Twelve-Step Programs teach people to access the support of a higher power rather than self-medicating discomfort. Spirit wants to help us, but we have to reach out first.

Addictions are sneaky. They strike fast when we are most vulnerable and overloaded. They are hard to resist with willpower alone. Here's how the spiritual process I'm suggesting works to center us. Let's say your father criticizes you and the hurt is intense. Or perhaps you're trapped in a group of energy vampires at work or overwhelmed by too much talking, light, or noise. In any of these scenarios, you just want relief. Instead of turning to a bottle of wine, a chocolate cake, or an expensive shopping spree, you can connect with a higher power to soothe your anxieties. Turning to our higher power calms us when we can't calm ourselves. It shifts us out of fear and into love. It brings us back to our heart, instead of leaving us spinning in a frenzy of agitation and worry. Turning to our higher power corrects our course.

Spirituality is your friend. It offers protection by enveloping you in the real power of goodness and love. Learning to go within to listen to Spirit gives you direct access, any time of the day or night, to the sense of peace and protection you deserve. Spirituality can be thought of as God, Goddess, nature, love, goodness, a compassionate universal intelligence, the power of your heart—whatever concept resonates with you. It links you to your intuition, which I believe is an extension of the divine. Although empaths are often highly intuitive, by regularly aligning with Spirit, you will further enhance your intuition. I strongly suggest you cultivate an active bond to Spirit by way of meditation, contemplation, prayer, being in nature, reading spiritual books, listening to sacred music, or attending Twelve-Step meetings.

The next time you're about to pick up a drink, overeat, or engage in another addiction, stop for a few minutes. Remember that the secret to overcoming cravings, fear, and anxiety is to shift out of your small addictive self and into your spiritual power. You can practice tuning in to your higher power with the following exercise. It can take you from an overwhelmed place into a much larger consciousness where you don't need to numb your sensitivities to feel okay.

PROTECTION STRATEGY
Open to a Higher Power

For at least five minutes each day, pause your busy life and cease all problem solving to connect to your higher power. Sit in a tranquil space, whether at home, in a park, in nature, or simply close your office door. Then, breathe deeply and slowly to relax your body. When thoughts intrude, picture them as clouds floating in the sky, coming and going. Do not attach to them. Keep returning to the rhythm of your breath.

In a still and calm state, inwardly invite in the presence of Spirit, however you define it. Spirit is energy. First look within you, not outside, then Spirit is easier to sense. Feel Spirit in your body and in your heart. Don't overthink it. Sense the warmth of love opening your heart and beginning to flow throughout your body. Feel your higher power—really get an energetic sense of it. Is it an experience of wholeness? An uplifting feeling? A sense that all is okay? Whatever you feel, savor this sensation. No rush. No pressure. Take time to let in the beautiful feeling. Once you get a sense of what your higher power feels like, you can reconnect with it again and again.

You can also ask for specific help from Spirit. For instance, "Please help me to stop taking on the anger of my bully-ing boss," or "Please lift my anxiety in social situations," or "Please help my partner understand my sensitivities." For optimal results, focus on one request per meditation. This makes the request more potent and makes it easier for you to track the results.

To conclude this meditation, say an inward "thank you" to Spirit and take a small reverent bow to honor this expe-rience. Then slowly and gently open your eyes. ■

Practice this meditation to find quick relief when you're over-whelmed. The more you connect with Spirit, the easier it will get. With this protection, you will feel safer and freer to soak up the positive energies in the world. One of the gifts of being an empath is being able to revel in heightened joy, compassion, peacefulness, and passion—experiences that nourish the soul. As we overcome addictions, we clear the way for feeling what is positive and beautiful in life.

To protect and center myself, I connect with Spirit many times a day to make sure my conscious contact is alive and well. Sometimes it's a ten-second check-in, but it can be longer, depending on my schedule. In addition, I practice other protection strategies, such as the Three-Minute Heart Meditation I shared in chapter 2. I also take alone time to regroup, and when I'm home, I jump into my bathtub with Epsom salts to release stress. I also use shielding to keep another person's energy from affecting me, and I walk in nature to feel the beauty there. I encourage you to regularly use the protection techniques I recommend throughout this book as well. They will help enhance your physical, emotional, and spiritual health, especially if you're struggling with an addiction.

> THE SPIRIT WITHIN ME
> IS GREATER THAN ANY
> ADDICTION OR FEAR.
> I AM NOT MY FEAR.
> I AM LARGER.
>
> Judith Orloff, MD

THE EMPATHIC EATER: FOOD, WEIGHT, AND OVEREATING

In my psychiatric practice, I've observed that overeating and food addictions are common among empaths. Food is medicine. It can stabilize an empath's sensitive system, but it can also throw it off. Food addiction is an uncontrollable craving for excess food. Many diets and weight-loss programs that are not spiritually based typically don't have enduring success with these overeaters. The specific addiction is often to sugar or carbohydrates. In contrast, periodic overeating is less severe and less addictive, though still a health hazard.

Why can food addiction and overeating be such a challenge for empaths? Let's look to early-twentieth-century faith healers for some answers. These women were often extremely obese. They claimed they needed to be heavy to protect themselves from taking on the pain and symptoms of their patients. Although this coping mechanism can be effective in that respect, there are other better options for self-protection that I'd like to share with you.

Excess weight is a way of armoring yourself against absorbing other people's stress. Added pounds can make you feel more grounded and buffer negativity. But reaching for sugar, carbohydrates, or junk foods for a quick fix is a short-lived and unhealthy solution that becomes addictive. Perhaps you have an empathic eating disorder that involves binging and purging. People do this in part to release negative energy from their system, though most aren't conscious of that motivation. Diets often fail for sensitive people who are unaware that they are eating and overeating unhealthy foods to protect themselves from overwhelming or negative energy. When I point this out to overweight empaths, it can be a life-changing insight for them.

You may relate to the tendency to reach for food to cope with sensory overload. If you're thin, you're especially vulnerable to absorbing distress of all kinds. However, there is a better solution. Practicing the protection strategies in this book—as I do, and I'm thin—will stop you from taking on the world's maladies. The solution to being an empathic eater is to find grounding and protection in healthier ways, including making the proper food choices.

SELF-ASSESSMENT   **Are You a Food Empath?**

- Do you overeat when you are emotionally overwhelmed?

- Do you turn to sugar, carbs, and junk food to self-soothe?

- Are you highly sensitive to the effect food has on your body?

- Do you get mood swings, brain fog, or feel toxic from sugar, caffeine, sodas, or junk food?

- Do you have food allergies and intolerances, such as to gluten or soy?

- Do you feel more protected from stress when you are heavy?

- Do you feel energized by healthy, clean food?

- Are you sensitive to the preservatives in food?

- Do you feel more vulnerable to stress when you are thin?

Here's how to interpret this self-assessment:

- Answering yes to one to three of the questions indicates you have some tendencies of a food empath.

- Answering yes to four to six of the questions indicates you have moderate tendencies toward being a food empath.

- Answering yes to more than six of the questions indicates you are a food empath, using food to self-medicate stress and discomfort.

Empaths have highly sensitive systems that need to be respected. We can react more strongly to food than other people. Because food is energy, empaths can feel the nuances of how different foods affect their bodies. So it's vital to make conscious food choices for your constitution.

I've treated some patients who have chosen to become vegans because they say they can feel the pain of slaughtered animals in their bodies. Because of an empath's highly tuned responses to food, it's important to notice what triggers your overeating and then practice the strategies below to help stay grounded without turning to food.

> EXCESS WEIGHT IS A WAY OF ARMORING YOURSELF AGAINST OTHER PEOPLE'S STRESS. LEARN TO PROTECT YOUR SENSITIVITIES IN HEALTHIER WAYS.
>
> **Judith Orloff, MD**

Ten Guidelines for the Empathic Eater

If you are an empathic eater, you will need to pinpoint the energetic stressors that trigger your overeating, such as a draining coworker, an argument, or feeling rejected. Train yourself to clear the energy as soon as possible to balance your system. Here are some tips to release negativity before you resort to overeating:

1. **Breathe the stress out of your body.** When you feel stress, immediately focus on breathing slowly and deeply. This releases negative energy. When we hold our breath out of fear, we trap toxicity in the body.

2. **Drink water.** Drink filtered or mountain spring water when you feel negative energy and have the urge to overeat. Water washes away impurities of all kinds. Drink at least six glasses daily to keep flushing out toxins. Also, take a bath or a shower to release negative energy.

3. **Limit your sugar intake.** Although you may crave sugar and carbs, as well as alcohol, they will destabilize you and cause mood swings, making you more susceptible to absorbing unwanted stress.

4. **Eat protein.** Protein stabilizes the nervous system and gives empaths a sense of grounding. It's optimal to have small protein meals four to seven times a day. This regimen will help you feel energetically stronger, safer, and more anchored in the world. If you are vegan, getting enough protein is crucial. I graze on small protein meals throughout the day, portions of lean protein snacks such as humanely raised chicken, grass-fed organic beef, or wild-caught fish. When I travel, this diet is harder to maintain, so I bring protein snacks with me, such as nuts, turkey jerky, or packets of protein powder that I mix with water. I won't lose my energy or grounding this way.

5. **Don't let your blood-sugar level drop.** Empaths are extremely sensitive to hypoglycemia. If you combine a busy life with low blood sugar, you're bound to get overwhelmed. So don't skip meals,

especially if you're going to be in a crowded place, traveling, or in business meetings. An empath with low blood sugar is a setup for exhaustion and overwhelm.

6. **Eat lots of vegetables.** If you tend to overeat and gain weight, eat lots of vegetables to fill yourself up and limit your cravings. You can also include some whole grains, but be careful about overdoing these and triggering a carb addiction.

7. **Healthy fats are good for you.** Good fats don't make you fat. Rather, they are a source of long-term energy throughout the day that keeps you from getting too hungry and resorting to binging. Be sure to include olive oil, coconut oil, and various nut oils in your diet. And don't forget foods high in omega-3 fats, such as salmon, omega-3 eggs, and flaxseed. Avocados, nuts, and beans are also good sources for healthy fats. I made the mistake of consuming a low-calorie, low-fat, low-carb diet and lost the energy boost that good fats provide. Research now shows that eating the right kinds of fats can even help us lose weight. It's the bad fats we want to avoid, such as the trans fats found in hydrogenated oils and packaged foods, which clog arteries and make us ill.

8. **Limit your caffeine intake.** Empaths are often sensitive to caffeine. I love drinking my one cup of coffee a day, but coffee can overstimulate me, so I

don't overdo it. If you feel you need two cups, you might try mixing caffeinated and decaffeinated coffee. Many empaths find that a small amount of caffeine increases their ability to buffer negative energies, but too much can make us jittery, tired, and vulnerable to picking up symptoms and stress. Be careful not to abuse caffeine, which is also found in soft drinks. In fact, it's wise to completely avoid soft drinks because of all the sugar they contain. Herbal and decaffeinated teas have calming properties, particularly chamomile, and can modulate feelings of overload.

9. **Eat for energy.** Organic, fresh, unprocessed, locally grown, non-GMO foods provide the most energy. Test various foods to see which give you lasting energy and which don't. I call this "eating with attunement." Sometimes when we're in highly positive energy environments, such as at inspirational workshops or conferences, our appetite can increase, so it's vital to eat the right foods. In my weekend intuition workshops, people tend to get much hungrier since they are meditating more and exploring new kinds of healing modalities. Food can ground the body so we can process more energy. Sense how different foods feel in your body, and stick to the ones that give you a healthy boost. This will help you avoid food addiction. The bottom line is that the better you feel, the less the world can deplete you. Empaths with clean diets are generally healthier, stronger, and less fragile.

EMPATHS FLOURISH ON ALIVE FOODS

Foods that are alive feel energetically different in our bodies than those that are dead. Since empaths are so sensitive to energy, we feel the difference between alive and dead foods. Here's how to intuitively tune in to the life force content of different foods so that you can choose those that nurture your body and prevent food addictions.

Alive foods have a glow. They're fragrant, delicious, energizing, organic, and free of chemicals and preservatives. There's no desire to overeat them. Alive foods give us pure energy, which feels balancing. Compare the energy and taste difference between homegrown tomatoes and the mass-produced ones that many markets carry. Train yourself to eat the alive foods that support your sensitive system.

Dead foods have a dull or tired look. They lack fragrance, they're unsatisfying, and they sap our energy or add none. They contain preservatives and chemicals or are enriched. Dead foods make us bloated or sick, cause brain fog, and stimulate sugar and carbohydrate binges. So be wary of dead foods and avoid them.

10. **Get tested for food allergies.** Empaths are prone to chemical sensitivities and food allergies, such as to gluten, soy, or yeast. Have a physician check to see if you have food allergies or gluten sensitivity, which is done through simple blood and saliva tests. If necessary, you can then eliminate these elements from your diet. Doing so will increase your energy and decrease inflammation in your body, including in your gut,

which will help heal irritable bowel syndrome or other causes of gastrointestinal distress.

In addition to the above ten guidelines, practice the following protection technique to ward off the desire to overeat when you're stressed.

PROTECTION STRATEGY
Keep a Meditation Pillow in Front of Your Refrigerator

If you use extra weight to protect yourself and are prone to food addiction, try keeping a meditation pillow in front of your refrigerator. Whenever you feel like overeating, this visual cue can stop you from opening the refrigerator door, reminding you to meditate instead.

Rather than reaching for food, sit on the pillow and close your eyes. Take a few breaths to center yourself. Identify what triggered your urge to overeat. Was it an angry relative? A feeling of loneliness? Are you overloaded after being around too many people? Did going to a shopping mall exhaust you? Be gentle with yourself. When obsessive thoughts to overeat intrude, visualize love flooding your body. Feel satiated by the nourishing love that is dissolving your fears and discomfort. Enjoy this feeling of self-soothing. You have the power to stabilize your mood and energy level in meditation. Inhale and exhale completely, and know that all is well. ■

Food can be a source of energy or depletion. You want to develop dietary habits that serve your sensitivities rather than aggravating them. Then you can maximize the energy you receive from food and minimize the protective defense mechanism of empathic overeating. With tools to protect and ground yourself, you won't have the same cravings that used to undermine your best intentions.

Following the suggestions in this chapter will make you healthier. It's important for empaths to evaluate their relationship to food and health and any tendency toward addictions. When we nurture our own well-being, we feel more protected from sensory overload, which safeguards against addictive behaviors.

EMPATH AFFIRMATION

I will listen to the wisdom of my body. I will eat a healthy diet. I will practice self-care to heal my addictions and stay physically, emotionally, and spiritually balanced.

Chapter 4

EMPATHS, LOVE, AND SEX

E mpaths often have special challenges in intimate relationships because of their intense sensitivities. Intimacy stretches our hearts so that we can become more loving and open people who honestly express our needs. To flourish in intimate relationships, empaths must learn to communicate authentically and set clear boundaries so that they feel at ease and don't get overloaded.

The right love relationship empowers empaths. Being valued and adored makes us more grounded. When empaths have an emotionally available partner who honors their sensitivities, they feel secure and supported. Despite the many amazing gifts of intimacy, however, too much togetherness can be difficult and result in sensory overload for empaths. As a result, relationships may feel very emotionally demanding and make some of us want to run. Why? As sensitive people we may unknowingly take on our partner's emotions and stress, and we can fear being suffocated in the relationship if we don't know how to set boundaries.

So here's our struggle: we want companionship, but it can feel unsafe. Empaths, myself included, often have the conflicting desires of wanting to be loved and wanting to be alone. We want to be needed, but we don't want other people's needs to burden us. We want to have a rich inner life, but we also want companionship. Shutting down, repressing our anxieties, walking on eggshells, or running away when these issues surface isn't the answer. What is? Learning to navigate and protect our sensitivities as well as setting clear limits with a partner. In this chapter, I will show you the way.

THE SEARCH FOR A SOUL MATE: ARE YOU ATTRACTED TO UNAVAILABLE PEOPLE?

In my workshops and psychiatric practice, I'm always struck by how many sensitive people want a long-term intimate relationship, and yet, despite their sincere efforts to date, their willingness to be fixed up or to join like-minded social groups, they remain single or keep being attracted to "unavailable" people.

I can relate to this. I've gone through long periods of time yearning for a partner. My pattern was that I'd fall in love with a man for a few good years, but ultimately the relationship wouldn't last. I treasure the comfort and passion of companionship, but it has taken me a long time to become at ease with authentically speaking my empath needs—and I am still learning! So I'd often end up feeling overwhelmed and bolt because I didn't know how to manage my sense of overload. Plus, I do a lot of emotional processing about a relationship when I am alone so I can be more present and less conflicted when I'm with my partner—though I didn't realize how important this was for me until recently. Then I would return to being single, which felt lonelier but less emotionally demanding because I didn't have to deal with someone else's needs. I've had to become extra compassionate with myself not to judge my low threshold for sensory overload in a relationship.

Even now, no matter how much I love and respect my partner (or anyone), if I'm around someone too much, I become overstimulated. The person will get on my nerves, and I'll start to feel anxious. As an empath, my challenge has been to balance my alone time with the time I spend with my partner. It takes a caring partner to walk us through this as we find a happy medium, and on those days when a happy medium isn't possible, to just leave me alone. I thank my partner for

> AS AN EMPATH, I HAVE
> BEEN STRUGGLING
> WITH WANTING LOVE
> VERSUS WANTING TO BE
> ALONE MY ENTIRE LIFE.
> **Judith Orloff, MD**

his understanding. Empaths aren't always easy to live with. Taking a break is essential for an empath's sanity. Those close to us must appreciate this.

Why can it be so difficult for empaths to find a soul mate? Is it just that there aren't enough "available" people out there, or is it that we're neurotic? No. In my own life, and in my psychotherapy practice, I've found another contributing factor. Discovering that I am a relationship empath has provided a major missing piece. Empaths are sensitive, intuitive, and caring, but since we're also shock absorbers with finely tuned nervous systems, we can react strongly. The marvelous part of being so sensitive is that we are in sync with our partner's emotions, sometimes even telepathically, and are sensual, responsive lovers—but the hard part is that we take on another person's stress. The closer we grow to someone, the more our sensitivities are heightened. So in romantic relationships, empaths are often drained or overloaded by the added stimulation that comes with togetherness. This differs from ordinary empathy—say, when we sympathize with a partner's bad day at work—because empaths actually merge with our partner's joy or sadness, as if it were our own. Thus, romantic relationships, particularly live-in ones, test us.

If you are an empath who hasn't identified this dynamic of absorbing your partner's stress, you may subconsciously avoid romantic relationships or be attracted to unavailable people. This could very well reflect your fear of getting overwhelmed. Here's the dynamic: a part of you wants a soul mate, but another part is afraid of being drained, trapped, or losing yourself. The closer you are to someone, the more intense your empathy and also your anxieties become. That's why empaths may often choose unavailable people. Unavailable people will never let an empath get close enough to experience their fears of intimacy. For example, empaths may have online relationships that never manifest or pick people who are ambivalent about love and give mixed messages. They keep wanting a connection that they'll never have. Sometimes empaths are attracted to what I call "new relationship addicts," or they themselves are the new relationship addicts. They enjoy the high of the honeymoon phase in a relationship but leave when intimacy sets in because it feels too overwhelming.

THE DIFFERENCE BETWEEN CONNECTION AND ATTACHMENT

Empaths often become attached to the wrong people because they see their "potential" and want to bring out the best in them. They reason, "This person just needs love, and then they'll open their heart to me." Empaths are very compassionate so it's easy to understand such an assumption, but it's generally not realistic. A healthy connection is when partners are mutually committed to the relationship and both want to open their hearts to each other. In contrast, attachment is when we cling to someone with a death grip, hoping that person will change. Attachments are dangerous because they can keep us linked to unavailable people or toxic relationships. If you are looking for intimacy, search out people who are excited to be with you.

Some of my empath patients have felt a strong soul mate connection with someone but then get confused when that "soul mate" isn't available and doesn't reciprocate their feelings. What these empaths are sensing is real, but the feelings might be from another time and place, as those who believe in past lives would say. Being together may not manifest in current time. The trap is when they become attached to the person and experience unrequited love. Time passes as they keep waiting for love to manifest. But it rarely does. The rule I teach my patients is that if a relationship is meant to be, it will definitely happen. Don't put yourself on hold for a person who is unattainable now.

FEAR OF COMMITMENT

Although I've had live-in relationships, I still have never married. Why not? I've pondered this often. On a deep level, I'm afraid of getting trapped in the wrong relationship without an escape hatch, and my fear as an empath is that I would give up too much of myself, with my needs getting squashed. That would feel like a kind of death to me. I look back at my old journals from 1988 in which I bemoaned (even back then) why I couldn't find a partner, let alone someone who would respect my great need for solitude.

I've learned that being an empath requires ongoing creative and honest conversations with your mate. As my Daoist teacher says, "Your soul mate can become your cell mate" if both of you are not dedicated to mutual growth and authenticity. It's painful to be in a relationship where communication isn't a priority. Then the one you love the most can seem like the enemy. A lack of mutual understanding just isn't viable for empaths if we want to feel good.

Now, I'm more open to voicing my needs, and my partner is open to listening. He's not afraid of my intense emotions, which makes me feel safe. I've always been wary of being "too intense" with men for fear of rejection.

To be comfortable enough to let go with a partner, sensitive people must first identify whether they are relationship empaths. If they are, they can set appropriate boundaries and assert their needs. That's when intimacy becomes possible.

SELF-ASSESSMENT **Am I a Relationship Empath?**

To determine whether you are a relationship empath, answer the questions in this self-assessment:

- Do I absorb a partner's stress, symptoms, and emotions?
- Am I afraid of being smothered or of losing my identity in close relationships?
- Does too much togetherness make me anxious?
- Do I need to be alone to recharge myself?
- Do I sometimes prefer sleeping alone?
- Am I annoyed by the sound of my partner watching television or talking on the phone when we're together?
- Are my feelings easily hurt?

- Do arguments make me ill or leave me exhausted?
- Do I have difficulty setting boundaries and asserting my needs?
- When my partner and I travel, do I prefer getting adjoining rooms?

Here's how to interpret your answers:

- Answering yes to one to two questions indicates that you have some of the tendencies of a relationship empath.
- Answering yes to three to six questions indicates that you have moderate relationship empath tendencies.
- Answering yes to seven or more questions indicates you have strong relationship empath tendencies and need to learn skills to manage your sensitivities in order to have a successful relationship.

CHOOSING WISELY: FINDING AN EMOTIONALLY COMPATIBLE PARTNER

Once you recognize that you are a relationship empath, you are ready to remove the obstacles to finding a nurturing partnership. Where do you start? Be prepared to reinvent what it means to be a couple and to release old stereotypes of what a marriage or being with an intimate partner looks like.

In a soul mate relationship, both people are dedicated to their own and the other's growth. A soul mate isn't perfect, and we can have many over a lifetime. My Daoist teacher says that when choosing who we get involved with, we must decide which set of problems we're most okay handling! But whether a relationship lasts two months, two years, two decades, or a lifetime, it has the ability to teach us to open our hearts and heal wounds in ourselves.

Empaths and their partners must decide how much time they want to spend with each other to make sure they are compatible. I have a patient who just spends the summers and holidays with her partner, which works out well for them because their kids are out of school then as well. Some couples prefer long-distance relationships and are happy to see each other on weekends. Some of my empath patients like being married to doctors, lawyers, pilots, or someone who frequently travels so that they can have more time alone or with their friends. It's often overwhelming for empaths to be with someone who works at home if they're at home too. Also, empaths like their partners to lead full lives, with friends, hobbies, time for exercising, and other interests; otherwise, empaths can be depleted if they are their partner's only significant contact. The hours spent away from an empath are often the saving grace of the relationship. There is no right or wrong about the amount of time partners spend together. I wholeheartedly urge you to find an arrangement that is most comfortable for you.

Who makes the best partners for empaths? In my book *Emotional Freedom,* I discuss three main emotional types that people fall into, though some of us are a mix. Knowing your soul mate's type provides insight into your interactions with each other. It will also help you master your emotions instead of simply reacting when your partner pushes your buttons (which soul mates are known to do!). Mastering your emotions doesn't mean repressing your feelings or experiencing them less.

Rather, it's about finding balance, healing your weak spots, and maximizing your strengths.

So how do you find a partner who is compatible with you? Empaths feel a soul connection with someone that's more about energy than words. Be aware of the way you relate to a person's energy. Notice whether the person's words match their energy. Or is something amiss? Are you shutting down for no apparent reason? Empaths often freeze around inauthentic people. Is your intuition saying to be careful or that something doesn't feel right? If you have doubts about whether a person's words, actions, and energy are congruent, go slowly. Do not give your heart to people unless they show themselves to be worthy of your love. Keep intuitively tuning in to find out who that person really is.

What kind of person is the ideal match for empaths? This depends on your temperament and needs. You must determine what type or mixture of types you prefer and will be most compatible with over time. Each of the types listed below can be extroverted or introverted.

Type 1. The Intellectual, or Intense Thinker

Intellectuals are astute analyzers who are most at home in their mind. They see the world through logic and rational thought. Known for keeping calm during a conflict, they often avoid their emotions, don't easily trust their gut, and are slow to participate in lighthearted or sensual activities. Intellectuals make good partners for certain empaths because their sense of logic complements and anchors the empath's emotional intensity.

TIPS TO HELP AN EMPATH COMMUNICATE WITH AN INTELLECTUAL

- **Ask for help.** Intellectuals love to solve problems. Be very specific about ways they can assist you with a problem or task. Then they will know exactly how to help.

- **Mention only one issue at a time.** Intellectuals can get thrown off by too many "unfixable" emotions. For instance, tell your partner that as an empath you need alone time after a busy day to recharge yourself. Make sure you convey that it's not personal, that they didn't do anything wrong.

- **Regularly communicate.** Keeping the lines of communication open with an intellectual allows you to be clear and loving with each other.

TIPS TO HELP AN INTELLECTUAL COMMUNICATE WITH AN EMPATH

- **Breathe.** If you are stuck in your head, practice "box breathing." Simply inhale deeply through your nose to the count of six, hold the breath for three counts, and then exhale through your mouth to the count of six. Repeat this a few times. It will relax you, quiet your thoughts, and make you more present with your empath partner.

- **Exercise.** Whether you're walking, swimming, or
  working out in a gym, exercise increases your body
  awareness, which quiets agitated or busy thoughts.
  It also relaxes you, making you calmer when you're
  with your partner. Yoga is also an excellent way for
  intellectuals to let go and just be, which an empath
  will appreciate.

- **Empathize.** Before addressing an empath's
  emotional issue, ask yourself, "How can I respond
  from my heart, not just my head?" And don't try
  to "fix" an empath's dilemma too quickly.

Type 2. The Empath, or Emotional Sponge

Empaths are kind, supportive, and passionate partners. They
also feel both their own and their spouse's emotions to an
extreme. I am often asked, "Can two empaths have a good relationship?" Yes, definitely. The heart connection is incredible.
Because both partners understand each other, they don't have
to explain themselves as much. However, for such a relationship to succeed and remain harmonious, the couple must keep
sharing about their mutual needs. Two empaths on overwhelm
at the same time can get pretty intense. A relationship between
such sensitive people requires mutual understanding and separate spaces where each can wind down.

I've treated many couples where both partners are empaths.
I've taught them how to respect each other's sensitivities while
staying grounded. The benefit of this relationship is that each
person easily appreciates what the other is feeling. The more difficult aspect is defining one's own needs and setting boundaries

to feel safe and calm. When empaths are triggered, they need a timeout to regroup and decompress. Two overwhelmed empaths can aggravate each other's anxiety. Each partner needs a separate quiet space to unwind. Though it is often challenging for two empaths to be in love, over the long term, the relationship can be successful.

TIPS TO HELP TWO EMPATHS COMMUNICATE

- **Take time apart each day to relax.** Minibreaks on one's own are calming and restorative. Go for a walk outside or meditate alone in your room. Focus on exhaling pent-up emotions, such as anxiety or fear, so they don't stay in your body. Afterward both partners can be clear and more present with each other.

- **Protect your sensitivities.** It's important for each partner to make a list of their top five emotional triggers. Then, together you can formulate a plan for handling these so neither of you gets caught in a panic. For instance, each partner can agree to drive their own car to events so that neither feels trapped in social situations when one is ready to go home before the other is.

- **Meditate together.** This helps both partners to connect spiritually in silence and will strengthen their bond.

Type 3. The Rock, or Strong and Silent Type

Consistent, dependable, and stable, this type of partner will always be there to lean on. Empaths can express emotions freely around them. Rocks won't get alarmed or be critical. They can be counted on, which is reassuring for empaths, who love consistency. But Rocks often have a hard time sharing their own feelings. Their empath mates may keep trying to get them to open up but become frustrated with the slow progress. Empaths may feel that Rocks are emotionally shut off, or even boring.

Empaths and Rocks can make wonderful partners. They balance each other. Rocks can learn from empaths how to express their emotions and passion more clearly, while empaths can learn to be grounded from the Rock. It's not that Rocks don't have feelings; it's that they need loving support to bring them out. Their feet are solid on the earth.

TIPS TO HELP AN EMPATH COMMUNICATE WITH A ROCK

- **Express gratitude.** Regularly voice appreciation for a Rock's positive qualities. Rocks light up when they're affirmed for what they genuinely contribute to a relationship.

- **Make an intimacy request.** In order to connect more deeply, ask the Rock to express at least one emotion a day, such as "I'm delighted," "I love you," or "I'm feeling anxious."

- **Spend time in nature together.** This gives both partners a mutual physical activity, which will bring the two of you even closer to each other in natural settings.

TIPS TO HELP A ROCK COMMUNICATE WITH AN EMPATH

- **Stir things up.** Initiate emotional exchanges so that you're not simply responding to your partner's lead.

- **Show your feelings.** Remember that expressing emotions is a form of passion and generosity.

- **Make physical contact.** Hug or put your arm around your partner—empaths love that!

I do best with a partner who is a Rock and not an empath. My mate is grounded and can hear my emotions without getting swept away by them. Being with another empath would feel too overwhelming for me. I also prefer a partner who is quiet and contained rather than someone who talks a lot and shares his emotional states frequently.

MAKE SURE YOUR PARTNER RESPECTS YOUR SENSITIVITY

As an empath, your next step is to ask yourself whether a potential partner honors your sensitivities. While getting to know someone, share that you're sensitive and how that means you feel emotions strongly and value having time alone. The right person will understand, while the wrong person will criticize you for being "overly sensitive"—a clear sign that someone might not be right for you.

I advise my patients to screen the people they date for their sensitivity IQ. What is that? The following assessment will help you to understand.

~~~~~~~~~~

SELF-ASSESSMENT **Determine Your Partner's Sensitivity IQ**

- Do they treat you lovingly and respectfully?
- Do they care about other people and have close friends?
- Do they treat the parking lot attendant or food server well?
- Are love and friendship a priority in their life?
- Do they respond well when you set limits and boundaries?
- Are they kind to children and animals?
- Do they appreciate nature?
- Do they honor the earth and actively try to preserve it?
- Are they giving and unselfish most of the time?
- And most importantly, are they capable of love?

Here's how to interpret your results:

- Seven to ten yeses indicate your potential mate has a high sensitivity IQ—which is good.

- Three to six yeses indicate a moderately high
  sensitivity IQ.

- Anything less than three indicates a low sensitivity
  IQ. This person's ability to be a sensitive partner is
  questionable, unless they get coaching or therapy to grow.

- Zero yeses are a sign for you to run in the opposite
  direction and find a more emotionally aware partner.

Not all empaths want or need to be in long-term soul mate relationships—and that's okay. It's not everyone's path to be part
of a couple. Growth can come in many other satisfying ways.
Sometimes empaths need a break from relationships to be with
themselves to grow and heal—which is also fine. One empath
told me, "I've been happily single for three years. I tend to put
others first and ignore my own needs in a relationship, so eventually I become unhappy. I feel more empowered when I'm single
because relationships can throw me off center. But I do want to
get to a point where I can feel empowered in a relationship."

HOW EMPATHS CAN HAVE
EMPOWERED INTIMATE PARTNERSHIPS

Research has shown that sensitive people are more likely than
others to be single, divorced, or separated, and less likely to have
ever been married. One interpretation of this information is
that empaths and sensitives tend to have special needs that make
marriage more challenging for both them and their partners.

But if you do want intimacy, how can you create an
empowered partnership? I can't emphasize enough the importance of authentic conversations about your empathic needs.

Compromise is key. Listen to your partner's desires too so that you can both find balance. The last thing you want is to feel pressured to be someone you're not. Empaths thrive on consistency, which fosters trust and acceptance. As one empath told me, "My husband accepts me exactly as I am. Through his acceptance, I have learned to be true to myself."

Empaths will have issues to resolve in relationships no matter how good the match. If you're embarking on or have been in a long-term relationship, here are some points to discuss with your partner about how to love an empath—and the common challenges and adjustments necessary to create a successful relationship.

> EXPRESS YOUR EMPATHIC NEEDS. IT'S TOO PAINFUL TO DENY YOUR OWN SENSITIVITIES TO MAKE OTHER PEOPLE COMFORTABLE.
>
> Judith Orloff, MD

TWELVE SECRETS FOR THE EMPATH IN LOVE

1. Value regular alone time to decompress and meditate

For an empath, having alone time in a relationship is about self-preservation. It's not just a luxury, so balance alone time with people time. Regularly take what I call a "golden hour" to decompress. Also get in the habit of having many minibreaks throughout the day. Tell your partner how vital this is for you because empaths need to think and process alone to regroup. This timeout gives you space to internally work through issues about the relationship too, so you have more clarity later with your partner. Sometimes you can have quiet time together—you don't want to be alone, you just want to be left alone. When you lovingly explain this to your partner, they're less likely to feel rejected or to take it personally. Make the matter about you and your own sensitivities rather than them.

There are ways to resolve the classic empath dilemma of needing alone time. When I was on a book tour and felt talked out after being with people all day, my partner would call me in my hotel room and we connected in silence. We'd just be quiet with each other on the phone. It was fantastic to do this with someone I love, not have to talk and yet still feel each other's presence. Although my partner and I adore each other and he's very caring, there are still empath issues to work out. I have a very strong hermit side, so we are finding our way. When we commit to an intimate partnership, the very nature of the relationship calls for sacrifice and compromise, but we don't want to compromise our soul. We must reach a balance.

2. Discuss how much time you want to spend socializing

Empaths, especially the introverted ones, have a more limited capacity for socializing than people who aren't empaths. We truly enjoy being alone in situations where others would prefer being social. One empath told me, "I would rather watch Netflix and order take-out than go to a party." Another empath shared, "I like people, but the loss of alone time is scary. It's like not being able to breathe. But too much free time leaves me feeling disconnected." Given this, try to reach a comfortable compromise about how much you socialize if your mate isn't an empath.

Here's what I did when I was on vacation with my partner in the Bahamas. We stayed at a bed and breakfast where everyone ate dinner together each night. He liked that and felt it was a good way to get to know interesting people. But I tend to be antisocial at times and don't enjoy small talk. Getting to know lots of strangers would drive me crazy. So we discussed what to do. One option was for me to eat alone in my room, which I normally would have done since that's what I'm comfortable with, but I didn't want to miss out on being with my partner. So we compromised. First, we ate dinner together on the dock, just the two of us. Then, he spent time afterward getting to know the other guests while I took some alone time. This compromise worked because we each got what we needed.

An empath I know in a similar situation told me that her fiancée liked sitting at the big social tables when they were on a cruise. Crowded cruises can be difficult for empaths, and she found this activity drained her. For a few days, when her fiancée became ill and stayed in his room, she dined alone and enjoyed it. Many people asked her to join them. "I guess they felt sorry for me," she said, "but I would politely decline. I love my own company. Very few people can understand that, but now my fiancée does."

3. Negotiate and make adjustments in physical space

Breathing room is essential. Decide what kind of space you need and establish some ground rules with your partner. Ask yourself what arrangement works best. Is it having a private area to retreat to, such as separate bathrooms (a must for me!), separate wings, apartments, or houses? Whatever you decide is fine as long as you agree not to crowd each other and avoid hovering close by. When traveling together, you may prefer adjoining rooms with your own bathrooms (I do). If sharing a room is the only option, hanging a sheet as a divider could help. A former boyfriend gave me the present of a Keep Out sign, which was perfect for me.

Also consider scents and chemical sensitivities in your environment since empaths have an acute sense of smell. Express your preferences. For instance, you may need to insist on no aftershave, perfumes, or synthetic body oils. Essential oils may be fine, but synthetic ones can be toxic to empaths.

4. Consider separate beds or bedrooms

Sleeping with someone else can be overrated. Most of us spend our childhoods sleeping alone, and then we're expected to share our beds as adults. That's a hard transition for many empaths. It's an expectation created by society that hurts those of us who don't fit into this stereotype. The assumption that spouses should always sleep in the same bed does not make sense to me. Indeed, in conventional relationships many partners enjoy sleeping together, but some empaths never get used to this. No matter how caring our partner is, we prefer our own space or maybe a king-sized bed or two twin beds pushed together. This way, both partners can stretch out on their side without touching the other. Give yourself permission to sleep in separate beds, have separate mattresses pushed together, or separate rooms if you need that.

Those who aren't empaths can feel lonely sleeping alone, so compromise when possible. For instance, you may decide to sleep together four nights a week and alone three. One empath I know talked to her partner about loosening the "snuggle hold" during sleep. She needed not to be held so close all night. Empaths don't always like constant cuddling. Another woman I know had a different solution to this problem. She sleeps on the "outside" when spooning with her husband. She finds the exchange of energy wonderful. But when she has had enough, she simply rolls back to her side of the bed to finish the night on her own. This approach ensures that she isn't stuck on the edge of the bed without much room.

Empaths tend to be light sleepers. A partner's snoring or thrashing around can easily disturb us. We may also need more sleep than our mates, and we get thrown off when our dream cycle is interrupted too. For years I slept alone for all of these reasons. But my current partner asked me if he could help me get used to sleeping with him through desensitization. I decided to try this. So at first he slept way over on the other side of the king-sized bed and agreed to move to another room if this didn't work for me. He said, "If it's uncomfortable, just touch me, and I will leave. If you decide that you want more contact, tell me and I'll move closer." Over time, this helped me feel more at ease sleeping together—although he is mostly a quiet sleeper and stays on his side of the bed. Still, if he gets too close and I want more space, I ask him to move over, and he does.

Some empaths like staying up late because the only time they can be alone is when their mate and kids are asleep. If you can relate, share your need for this arrangement with your partner so that they understand.

5. Focus on a single emotional issue, and don't keep repeating yourself

Empaths can have many emotional issues going on simultaneously, which may be overwhelming for them and their partners. The best way to communicate with your mate is by sharing one issue at a time, without repeating it, unless you're asked for clarification. My partner says he feels like his brain is being squeezed when I raise too many dilemmas at once, or when I keep repeating myself to make a point. Men especially tend to be task-oriented, and they like to be helpful. Multiple requests for change in the same discussion make it all seem impossible. For instance, if you bombard your mate with "I'm furious about how my boss treated me" and then "My nerves are shot so please turn down the TV" and then "Will you help me bring in the groceries?" and finally "I need you to listen to me when I'm frustrated!" that is way too much for your partner to assimilate. Also remember that empaths need space to decompress after a conflict. So plan time alone to reset your rhythms, process your issues, and center yourself.

6. Don't take things personally, even when they are personal

This is an important but demanding principle on a spiritual path, yet it's basic to good communication and relationship harmony. Try to be less reactive to comments and more centered so that you aren't triggered as often or as intensely.

7. Use the Sandwich Technique: Make requests, not demands

Sandwich whatever you'd like your partner to change or a topic of conflict between two positive statements. Here's how this works. For example, first say, "I love you so much and appreciate your support!" Then put in your request: "I need your help with something. I would like to meditate for a half hour each night. It would be great if you could give me that private time. This will help me be even more present with you later." Then hug your partner and thank them for taking care of you in this way. Remember to use this helpful technique when you're raising difficult issues.

8. Observe the no-yelling rule

Empaths are overwhelmed by yelling and loud voices. Our partners need to accept this about us. For the sake of self-pres-ervation, I'm strict about this rule in my house. One empath told me, "I cannot stand arguing around me. The vibration of anger in my body feels like I'm being hit. If I'm in a yelling match, I'm drained for days."

9. Don't be a people pleaser or try to fix your partner

Empaths grow tired when we try to fix others' problems or try to please others at the expense of our own needs. So prac-tice loving detachment, and set boundaries. From the start, my partner told me he disliked getting instructions on self-improvement. When he's going through a hard time, he has trained me to say, "I have faith that you can handle it," rather than my offering suggestions he didn't ask for. This technique stops me from absorbing his stress—an essential survival skill for empaths in relationships—while it shows respect for his ability to handle his own problems. Try not to interfere in your partner's life. It's a gift to let others be themselves and face their own difficulties.

10. Modulate the sounds around you

Empaths are usually quiet people. Our loved ones must accept this about us and be sensitive about the kinds of sounds they bring into the home. Ask your mate to understand your need to have peace and quiet. If you can't tolerate a TV or radio on constantly, a headset or earplugs are fine solutions. You might want to keep computers out of bed as well because they produce glaring light, sound intrusions, and harmful electromagnetic radiation.

11. Negotiate your bath time

Empaths love being in water. We tend to take long baths and showers. In truth, I could soak for an hour or more every night. I am lucky to have a window in my bathroom so I can see the moonlight reflected in the water. This puts me in trance, which feels so rejuvenating. However, my partner enjoys me being in bed with him when we go to sleep. So we compromise. Some nights I take longer baths, and other nights I take shorter ones.

12. Play

Empaths tend to be serious, but we also love to play. Be playful with your partner, and let your beloved see your inner child.

SEXUALITY AND EMPATHS

Sexuality is an important topic for empaths to get clear about, whether we're single, dating, or in a long-term relationship. Because we are so sensitive to energy, there is no such thing as "casual sex." During lovemaking, energies combine. We can pick up both anxiety and joy from our sexual partner, and we often get intuitions about their thoughts and feelings. Therefore, choose your sexual partners discerningly. Otherwise, during lovemaking you could absorb stress, fear, or other toxic energy. This is particularly true if you are a sexual empath.

What is a sexual empath? Someone whose empathic abilities intensify during an erotic encounter so that they sense heightened bliss or stress. Sexual empaths are highly sensitive during flirting too. They pick up a partner's energy even more than other empaths do. For all empaths, especially sexual empaths, to feel their best, they must share physical intimacy with the right person, someone who can reciprocate love and respect.

Unfortunately, some of my empath patients have made mistakes when they've been without a partner for a long time. If someone comes along who sparks their sexuality, they are so eager to enter a relationship that they ignore the intuitive warning signs. So they engage in a sexual relationship early on with a person who is a poor choice for them. They often fear that because it has taken so long to find someone, they'd better get involved despite the intuitive red flags. But, of course, we open ourselves to hurt when we become overly attached to people who can't love us back. One empath told me, "I haven't been in a serious relationship for five years, but when I've dated men who I was fast and furious in love with, I turned into this love-crazed person. I didn't listen to the warning signs, and I was disappointed. But now, I go slower to make sure the person is available."

One solution to simply waiting for a partner to show up is to attend a Tantra workshop or to have a private session with a Tantric teacher. Tantra is an ancient Indian practice that combines sexuality and spirituality by way of body-centered exercises. Whether in a private or group setting, you will be taught to tune in to your body, tap in to your sexual and spiritual energies, and work through old traumas, destructive relationship patterns, or numbness that stops you from feeling. These sessions increase sexual energy and keep it flowing to maximize our powers of attraction, rather than allowing this energy to go dormant. Others may not feel how sexy you are if that happens.

A few years ago, I experienced some valuable Tantric sessions after I became involved with the wrong person too quickly. I wanted to address the blocks that contributed to my pattern of choosing unavailable men or having long periods alone. I was tired of talking about these issues with my psychotherapist, so instead, I chose these Tantric sessions, which helped me open blocked energy and attract a compatible partner.

Once you've found a partner who is a good match for you, the basis for intimacy is to combine your heart energies with your sexual energies. Empaths thrive on heart energy. When sexuality, spirit, and heart are combined in lovemaking, it is sublimely nurturing to your system.

Part of maintaining a heart-centered sexuality is learning to set limits with your partner if something about the interaction feels off. For instance, if your partner had a frustrating day and is angry, it might not be the best time to be sexual because an empath can absorb this anger. Have a frank conversation about all this. Your beloved needs to understand why you would choose not to be intimate when they are angry or especially stressed.

Educate your mate about your sensitivities. Unless you're in a relationship with an empath, you will need to lovingly explain your reactions so that your partner can meet your needs. The empath's universe is different from the universe of someone who is not an empath. Your compassion and patience will make all the difference in your closeness.

TREASURE YOUR RELATIONSHIP NEEDS

Empaths must strike a balance between energy going out and energy coming in. We have such big hearts that we often err on the side of giving too much to family, friends, spouses, and children. This wears us out. We help too much, we give too much, but we don't receive enough. Finding balance is of paramount importance for protecting our own energy. Both giving love and receiving love is the recipe for a fulfilling relationship.

Knowing your needs and being able to assert them is a strong form of self-protection for empaths. Then you can be in your full power in a relationship. If you're single, you can identify your needs now so that your vision is clear when you date someone or have a partner. If something doesn't feel right in a relationship, you can raise the issue with your mate rather than suffering silently. Finding your voice is equivalent to finding your power. Otherwise you may become exhausted, anxious, or feel like a doormat in relationships because your basic needs are unmet. Your partner isn't a mind-reader. So speak up to safeguard your well-being. The following exercise will support you with this.

PROTECTION STRATEGY
Define and Express Your Relationship Needs

Quiet your mind with slow and regular breaths. Feel the joy of having this time to listen to your deepest self as an empath.

Now ask yourself, *What do I need in a relationship that I've been afraid to ask for? Which of my sensitivities would I most like a partner to support? What would make me feel most comfortable with someone?* Inwardly pose these questions or others that surface for you. Then intuitively tune in to the answers rather than trying to figure them out. Listen to your body and its signals. Let any aha! feelings and intuitive insights flow. Take special note of those intuitions that make you feel more powerful and protected.

Stay open. Don't censor anything. Would you prefer more alone or quiet time? Would you like to sleep by yourself sometimes? Do you want to play more or talk more or have sex more? Let your intuition flow without judgment. Uncover your true feelings. There is no reason to be ashamed or to hold back. Focus on treasuring your needs as an empath. Compassionately accept all your quirks and sensitivities. Let this loving feeling inspire you to be authentic.

By defining what feels good for you (and what doesn't), you're keeping negative energy out and protecting yourself. Sit quietly for a few moments when you feel complete with this inquiry, and enjoy being immersed in the good feelings. ■

After you've finished with this meditation, record in a journal what you discovered about your relationship needs. If you're single, it's helpful to be aware of them, and if you're in a couple, gradually begin to express them so that your beloved will know better how to support you.

～

Good relationships are possible for empaths and can enhance our sense of security, love, and grounding. Marriage or any kind of sacred union needs to be a competition of generosity. This means that each partner is in service to the other, aiming to deepen their devotion, kindness, passion, and love every day. Relationship is a spiritual experience, where we can learn from each other, share our hearts, and take good care of each other. Consideration and tolerance are essential. Empaths will thrive in partnerships where these qualities are a priority and authentic communication is the goal.

EMPATH
AFFIRMATION

In a quiet state of self-acceptance,
tell yourself: I deserve to be in
a loving relationship where I feel
comfortable. I deserve to express
my true needs. I deserve to have
my sensitivities respected.
I deserve to be heard.

Chapter 5

PROTECTING YOURSELF FROM NARCISSISTS AND OTHER ENERGY VAMPIRES

Energy vampires are attracted to the openness and loving hearts of empaths. Sensitive people need to be prepared for them. I've found that some relationships are positive and energizing for my empath patients, but others are draining. In fact, certain people can suck the positivity and peacefulness right out of you. I call these drainers "energy vampires." At work, at home, or anywhere in your life, energy vampires drain your physical and emotional energy. The super toxic ones can make you believe you're flawed and unlovable. You may tiptoe around them for fear of an explosion. Some attack with put-downs, blame, or shame. They might say, "Dear, you're looking really tired and old today," or "You're too sensitive." Suddenly you feel as if something is wrong with you.

An essential action step in *The Empath's Survival Guide* is to identify the energy vampires in your life and develop strategies to effectively deal with them. Doing so will make a tremendous difference in the quality of your relationships and prevent you from being sapped by them. Don't let energy vampires take you by surprise. Create a plan. Try not to take their barbs personally, even when they are intentional. The effort to do this, though often strenuous, is necessary to take back your power and protect your sensitivities. Remember: these drainers are motivated by fear and insecurity. They annoy and deplete many people, not just you.

~~~~~~~~~~~~~~~~~~~~~~~~~~~~~~

SELF-ASSESSMENT **How do you know if you've met an energy vampire?**

Here are some signs to watch for:

- You feel tired and want to go to sleep.

- You're suddenly in a terrible mood.

- You feel sick.

- You don't feel seen or heard.

- You reach for sugar or carbohydrates for a boost.

- You start doubting yourself and become self-critical.

- You become anxious, angry, or negative when you didn't feel that way before.

- You feel shamed, controlled, or judged.

~~~~~~~~~~~~~~~~~~~~~~~~~~~~~~

Sometimes you might attract a specific type of energy vampire because of the mutual emotional issues you both need to heal. So you enter into an unhealthy "wound-mate relationship," where you keep repeating the wounding process with each other. There's an odd psychological comfort to this because it's what you both know, what you're used to. You become attached to a toxic person and can't let go. This keeps you stuck in a painful cycle. For instance, your low self-esteem attracts people who criticize you, and the criticizer attracts people they can belittle. Be careful not to perpetuate wound-mate relationships. Instead, let these people—whether they are friends, coworkers, spouses, or whomever—spur you to develop self-awareness and heal the initial wound. Then you can grow out of these relationships and find more fulfilling ones.

THE SEVEN TYPES OF ENERGY VAMPIRES

In over twenty years in my medical practice, I have identified seven main types of energy vampires to watch out for who are particularly dangerous for empaths.

1. The Narcissist

Of all the vampires, narcissists can be the most destructive to empaths. I'm referring to full-blown narcissists, not simply people with a few narcissistic traits (who may have more empathy). Let me explain. Narcissists act as if the world revolves around them. They have an inflated sense of importance and entitlement. They need to be the center of attention and require endless praise. You must compliment them to get their approval. They can also be extremely intuitive, but they use their intuition to manipulate and achieve their goals. They can do much damage to empaths because they have little or no capacity for unconditional love. If you don't do things their way or if you disagree with them, they become ice-cold and punishing, withhold love, or give you the silent treatment, which can last days or weeks.

Scientific research on narcissists (as well as sociopaths and psychopaths) has shown that they have an "empathy deficient disorder." Full-blown narcissists use what seems like empathy to get what they want when you begin to distance yourself. But their empathy is not reliable or real. Narcissists are persuasive charmers who know exactly what to say to emotionally seduce you. If you try to leave, they will sweet-talk you to get you back. But their "empathy" will last only as long as they need it to. There are always strings attached to the favors they bestow. Once you've returned, they'll revert to being self-absorbed again.

Why is there such a fatal attraction between empaths and narcissists? I've seen this destructive dynamic with numerous patients. Empaths must let the seriousness of getting involved with a narcissist sink in and understand what traits they keep being attracted to. Empaths get caught up in the narcissist's charisma and the promise of love and connection. Narcissists may appear to have so much to give—but they don't. The confusing part is that on the surface they can be smart, funny, thoughtful, and generous, but they can't maintain that front in intimate relationships.

> RESEARCH SHOWS THAT NARCISSISTS HAVE AN EMPATHY DEFICIT DISORDER. DO NOT TRUST THEM WITH YOUR HEART.
>
> Judith Orloff, MD

Empaths are targets for narcissists. Why? Because empaths are sensitive, attentive, innocent or even gullible, and are easy to drain because they lack the usual defenses most people have. It's hard for empaths to believe that narcissists don't possess a capacity for empathy because that's how we're wired, how we perceive the world. Empaths are compassionate and expect others to be the same, so they make the mistake of trying to win over a narcissist with love. I'm sorry to say: that won't work. It's like expecting someone without a heart to know how to love.

A big problem with getting involved with a narcissist is that it's hard to leave the relationship. I've seen it take decades for some people. One empath workshop participant told me, "I was married to a narcissist for ten years. It felt as if pieces of my soul were killed off a little bit at a time in the relationship. When I finally left, it practically destroyed me." She is *not* overstating this. Narcissists can make empaths feel physically ill and depressed. They can beat down self-esteem until empaths no longer believe in themselves. Narcissists don't make much progress in psychotherapy because they always blame the other person and have no accountability for their part in a conflict.

Narcissists sometimes use a harmful technique called gaslighting, which distorts another's perception of reality by intentionally setting up crazy-making situations and then questioning the person's sanity for reacting to the craziness. They also rewrite the past or deny an event took place, dismissing the other person's concerns as unfounded. The sad part is that many of their victims believe them.

PROTECTION STRATEGY
Protect Yourself from Narcissists

- **Lower your expectations for the narcissist's emotional capabilities.**

- **Don't let yourself be manipulated.**

- **Don't expect a narcissist to respect your sensitivities**—they are extremely cold people.

- **Don't fall in love with a narcissist.** Run in the opposite direction no matter how attracted you feel.

- **Try to avoid working with a narcissistic boss**—but if you can't leave, don't let your self-esteem depend on your boss's reactions.

- **Stroke the narcissist's ego.** Frame your request in terms of how it can benefit them. This is the only way you will get through to a narcissist. For instance, if you want to take a few days off to attend a work-related conference, tell your boss something like, "This will help me make your business more successful," rather than, "I need a break from the office." To successfully communicate and get the results you desire, show how your request will be to the narcissist's advantage.

- **Stop all contact when you can.** To end a relationship with a narcissist (or anyone with whom you want a complete break), go cold turkey. Keep moving, and never look back. In addition, use these strategies:

  ▲ **Practice a cord-cutting visualization.** In a calm state, picture cords of light connecting both of you. Inwardly say "thank you" for what you've learned from the relationship, even if the lessons were hard. Then firmly assert, "It's time to completely break our bonds." Next, visualize taking a pair of scissors and cutting each bond completely so that you're free of any energetic ties. This visualization will help you release the relationship and also remove lingering energy that you feel from the person.

▲ **Have honorable closure.** This shamanic technique lets you release a relationship, particularly if you keep thinking about the person or sense that they're thinking about you. Go out into nature and find a large stick. Look at the stick and declare, "This relationship is over." Then break the stick in half, leave the pieces on the ground, walk away, and never look back. This finalizes the ceremony of closure. ▪

2. The Rageaholic

This energy vampire deals with conflict by accusing, attacking, and controlling. Rageaholics often yell to make a point, and as I noted in chapter 4, empaths can't tolerate yelling. We actually feel physical pain when we're around yelling. Rageaholics usually behave most poorly around their loved ones. They say horrible things that they may regret later, such as, "You're a bad wife" or "I'm not attracted to you anymore." Such comments can tear through an empath's vulnerable heart. Rageaholics traumatize empaths by beating down their positivity and self-worth.

Empaths often experience sensory overload around yelling, arguments, loud noises, and loud personalities. That's why I don't allow any anger to be dumped in my vicinity. I was once waiting for a friend to finish a phone conversation. She became agitated and started yelling at the person she was talking to. It felt like that toxic energy was being deposited on me, and I suffered from the fallout of her anger. Later, I told her, "Look, I'm an empath. Your anger affects me, and I feel drained. Please don't do it again." Thankfully, she heard me, and never repeated that behavior.

I've actually left a lunch with friends when a man there got enraged with his spouse. His rage hurt me. In situations like that, I am fierce about protecting my energy, so I said to my friends, "Please excuse me. I'm feeling tired," and politely left. It was awkward, but I chose my well-being over "social correctness" and sticking it out.

An empath patient described his response to arguments to me: "I was having dinner at my girlfriend's house. Her family started screaming at one another at the table. I was horrified. She said, 'Oh, this is just how we talk to each other. It's normal.' I was exhausted, but I didn't know how to cope." Of course, many empaths would feel the same way. We need to recover from angry outbursts. Afterward, it's important to allow some quiet time to lower the stimulation level and then convey our needs to our loved ones.

When setting limits with a rageaholic, empaths must know the difference between venting and dumping. There are healthy ways to express anger, such as venting, which an empath can handle. There are also toxic ways to do so, such as dumping, which can traumatize empaths. For instance, if your spouse wants to express anger with you, ask them to make a request first by saying something like, "I have a request. I need to vent about an issue. Is that okay to do now?" This approach gives an empath some warning so that we're not hijacked. Then, it's your choice to discuss the issue right away or later, after you've had adequate time to feel centered and prepared.

Here are some guidelines for communicating anger, whether expressing your own feelings or listening to another's. Use these guidelines and share them with loved ones.

KNOW THE DIFFERENCE BETWEEN VENTING AND DUMPING

Venting feels healthy and is time limited. When venting,

- stick to one topic
- don't keep repeating the same point
- don't blame
- don't fall into victim mode
- be accountable for your own part
- stay open to solutions

Dumping feels toxic and goes on and on. Someone who is dumping

- overwhelms another with many issues
- keeps repeating the same point
- blames others
- plays the victim
- shows no accountability for their part in a matter
- is not open to solutions

In addition, you can use the following basic ground rules for expressing anger, making everyone feel safer and more protected. They are effective with rageaholics.

PROTECTION STRATEGY
Protect Yourself from Rageaholics

- **Let the rageaholic know you hear them.** Then suggest that the issue be worked out respectfully after they calm down. Say something like, "I want to help you, but it's hard for me to listen when you're in this state." Refuse to engage with their anger.

- **Set a "no-yelling" rule with loved ones.** At the very least, it's not allowed around you. There are other ways to resolve conflicts without yelling.

- **Stay calm.** Do not yell back when triggered. Reacting impulsively will just drain you and aggravate the situation.

- **Pause when agitated.** Count to ten. Take a timeout to quiet the fight-or-flight response. Wait until you're calm before you respond to someone's anger; otherwise, the angry person may dump more of it onto you.

- **Practice restraint with your speech in all its forms, including texting, email, and phone.** Then you'll be in charge of your emotions when you choose to address the person.

- **Visualize yourself as an open window with air freely flowing through it.** Similarly, let

someone's anger pass through the open window
so it doesn't get stuck in you.

- **Leave the room, or ask the person to leave if
  they won't stop yelling.** ▪

3. The Victim

Energy vampires with a victim mentality drain empaths with
their "the world is against me" attitude. They don't take responsibility for the problems that happen in their lives. Other people
are always the cause of their distress. Empaths often fall into
the compassionate caretaker role with "victims," trying to solve
their list of problems. Of course, this drains empaths. Victims
typically respond to any possible solution with, "Yes, but . . . "
So the empath may get frustrated and end up screening emails
or calls or purposely avoiding this draining person. Although
we want to be supportive, the victim's barrage of complaints is
too much for sensitive people to take. Empaths must learn to
assert boundaries with people who have a victim mentality and
be careful not to turn into a codependent or their "therapist."

PROTECTION STRATEGY
Protect Yourself from Victims

- **Set compassionate and clear boundaries.** People can hear
  us better when we're not being snippy or impatient.

- **Use the Three-Minute Phone Call.** Listen briefly,
  then tell your friend or family member, "I support

you, but I can only listen for a few minutes if you keep rehashing the same issues. Perhaps you could benefit from finding a therapist to help you."

- **Say "no" with a smile.** For instance, with a coworker, you can smile and say something like, "I'll hold positive thoughts for the best possible outcome. Thank you for understanding that I'm on deadline and must get back to my project." With friends and family, briefly empathize with their problem, but then say "no" with a smile by changing the subject and not encouraging their complaints.

- **Set limits with body language.** This is a good time to cross your arms and break eye contact to send a message that you're busy. ■

4. The Drama Queen or King

These types drain sensitive people by overloading them with nonstop dramas. These dramas impose too much information and stimulation for empaths to process. Their histrionics deplete us. Drama is a kind of drug that some people become addicted to. Don't enable that addiction. My patient Zoe was aggravated when a friend kept canceling their plans at the last minute with different excuses. Once he had a toothache and almost fainted. Another time his wallet was stolen, and he had to go to the police station. Then he had a minor car accident, without injury, but spent all day in the emergency room. Zoe was worn out by his dramatic episodes and tired of being stranded. Drama queens and kings get energized by our reaction to their drama, but they don't get rewarded when we remain calm. So, stay consistently calm. Soon they will lose interest and look for someone else who will feed their drama.

PROTECTION STRATEGY
Protect Yourself from Drama Queens or Kings

- **Don't ask these people how they are doing.**
  You don't want to know.

- **Breathe deeply.** When drama queens or kings start up, breathe deeply, stay calm, and do not get caught up in their story.

- **Set kind but firm limits.** For example, you might say to a friend who keeps canceling plans, "I'm sorry for all your mishaps, but let's not reschedule until things settle down for you and you can show up." Setting limits helps you communicate clearly and doesn't reinforce their behavior. ■

SMILE AND LAUGH MORE. IT WILL KEEP THE ENERGY VAMPIRES AWAY.

Judith Orloff, MD

5. Control Freaks and Critics

These energy vampires always offer their unsolicited opinions, such as, "You know what you should do . . . ?" Then they proceed to tell you, whether or not you want to hear their advice. Or they continue to nitpick about the things that you're "doing wrong," such as, "You forgot to put the dishes away, again," or "You really should learn to park better." Empaths may take to heart a control freak's disapproval, particularly if they lack self-confidence. So they end up feeling attacked, depressed, and tired. Remember that an opinion requires no accountability and is subjective. Of course, it can be helpful to listen to criticism, but if the comment isn't constructive or doesn't make sense, it's not helpful. In general, criticism, especially ongoing nitpicking, can drain empaths.

PROTECTION STRATEGY
Protect Yourself from Control Freaks and Critics

- **Be assertive, but don't tell these types what to do because that will only make them defensive.** Instead, say to them, "I value your advice, but I want to think about how to approach this situation myself."

- **Politely ask the person to stop criticizing you.** Be firm and nonemotional. Don't play the victim.

- **If you feel inadequate around a controller or a critic, identify the self-esteem issue that has been triggered and focus on healing it.** The more secure you feel, the less these vampires can hurt you. ■

6. The Nonstop Talker
Nonstop talkers can drain the life force out of empaths with an endless verbal assault. I try to avoid these people because they grate

on my nerves and sensitivities. They trap you and recount their life stories without pausing for a breath, and they don't give you any openings to interrupt them. They can also move in so close physically that they intrude on your personal space. You take a few steps backward, and they take a few steps forward. You can't escape. There's a joke that there needs to be a Twelve-Step Program for addictive talkers called "On and On and On Anonymous."

Empaths are incredible listeners but often make the mistake of tolerating chronic talkers for too long. Then we become exhausted. To protect ourselves, empaths must address our tendency to people please. Everyone loves telling empaths their life stories because we're so attentive. But with chronic talkers, we must learn to set boundaries, a basic form of self-care.

PROTECTION STRATEGY
Protect Yourself from Nonstop Talkers

- **Nonstop talkers don't respond to your nonverbal cues.** Simply looking impatient or restless doesn't work. You must interrupt them, as hard as this may be to do.

- **Be tactful.** Although you may really feel like saying, "Be quiet. You're driving me crazy," that would just make the person defensive or angry. Instead, smile and nicely say something like, "Please excuse me for interrupting, but I need to talk to someone else at this party," or "I have an appointment I must keep." A socially acceptable reason to leave that I often use is, "I have to go to the bathroom."

- **State a request.** With a family member or coworker, in a neutral and nonblaming tone let them know, "I'd like to add to the discussion too. It would be great if you would allow me to contribute." If you convey this message without irritation, you will be better heard.

- **Use humor.** With people you know well, who will understand, you can jokingly say, "The clock is ticking," as one good friend does with me when I get long-winded. ▪

7. Passive-Aggressive People

Passive-aggressive people express their anger with a smile. They sugarcoat hostility, but you can intuitively sense the anger beneath their pleasant facade. They often procrastinate, conveniently "forget," and make excuses for why they couldn't fulfill a commitment. These people seem so sincere, but they aren't dependable. They will promise you anything, but then do as they please. To make things even more difficult, narcissism and passive aggression can often be present in the same person, which is a double danger for empaths.

Here are some examples of passive-aggressive behavior. Your partner keeps forgetting your birthday, though they know how important celebrating is to you. A friend brings cupcakes to your house when she knows you are on a diet. Noisy neighbors promise to be quiet but aren't. A colleague keeps saying "I'll get back to you" about a mutual work project, but never does, making you chase after him. Passive-aggressive people are known for making sarcastic comments about you and then saying, "Can't you take a joke?" They also sulk when they don't get what they want but claim "nothing is wrong." These are confusing messages for empaths who are much more direct.

PROTECTION STRATEGY
Protect Yourself from Passive-Aggressive People

- **Don't question your response to a passive-aggressive person.** Just because their anger is so hidden doesn't mean it's not real. Trust your intuition.

- **Recognize the pattern and address the behavior with the person.**

- **Focus on resolving one issue at a time, so the passive-aggressive person doesn't feel attacked.** For instance, if a friend keeps saying "yes" to helping you with a task but doesn't, tell them in a neutral tone, "Please don't make a commitment if you can't follow through." Then notice how they respond. They might say, "I apologize. I have to be more focused." See if their behavior changes. If it doesn't, you can raise the issue again, or simply accept that this person is not dependable and stop making requests of them.

- **If you can't get a direct answer, ask the person to clarify their position.** It's important to address the behavior and find a solution. Being specific with someone who is passive aggressive will make them take a stand. ■

THE EMPATH'S SURVIVAL GUIDE

> YOU CANNOT SEEK
> WATER FROM THE
> ONE WHO DRAINED
> YOUR SEAS, AND
> YOU CANNOT BUILD
> A HOME FOR YOUR
> WORTH INSIDE OF
> ANOTHER BEING.
> THE MEDICINE IS
> WHEN YOU RETURN
> TO YOURSELF,
> WHERE YOU WILL
> REMEMBER YOUR
> STRENGTH, RECLAIM
> YOUR OWN RHYTHM,
> AND WRITE YOUR
> NEW SONG.
>
> **Victoria Erickson**

Use the above strategies to cope with the seven types of energy vampires in your life. Then you will have the power—not them. Take an inventory of people who give you energy and those who drain you. You can create separate lists for work, home and family, friends, and peripheral relationships. You might decide to completely stop having contact with some people who drain you. For those who must stay in your life, such as certain family members, decide what strategies to use and consistently implement them. Learning to set limits with emotional vampires will protect your sensitivities and enhance your well-being.

DEALING WITH AN EMOTIONAL HANGOVER

Although we may set excellent limits with energy vampires, it's still not uncommon for empaths to experience "emotional hangovers," an energetic residue left over from the interaction. Toxic emotions can linger long afterward, which makes us feel exhausted, beset with brain fog, or even ill. When dealing with energy vampires, empaths often need time to recuperate later. In addition, try the following suggestions to address these hangover symptoms.

PROTECTION STRATEGY
How to Cure an Emotional Hangover

- **Practice the shower meditation.** When showering, stand under the stream of water and say this affirmation, inwardly or aloud: "Let this water wash away all the negative energy from my mind, body, and spirit." Feel the shower cleansing you and rejuvenating you.

- **Use gemstones.** Carry or wear one of these stones—a black tourmaline, an amethyst, or a black obsidian—to help ground yourself and remove an emotional hangover. Shamans teach that if you carry or wear black, you will be more protected. I wear a jade pendant of Quan Yin, the Chinese expression of the goddess of compassion and a protector of goodness. I love how jade changes with my body chemistry and emotional shifts over the years.

- **Smudge your space.** In Native American culture, burning medicinal or aromatic plants, a technique called "smudging," clears negative and stagnant energy from a location. I love to burn sweetgrass. Its beautiful smell wafting through the air feels nurturing to my feminine essence. Sage is effective too. I also pick sprigs of cypress, eucalyptus, and juniper to burn. Experiment with the plant scents you respond to.

- **Use negative ion generators or salt lamps.** These devices produce negative ions, and negative ions clear the air of dust, mold spores, pollen, odors, cigarette smoke, bacteria, and viruses. They are also thought to remove leftover negativity in a home, an office, or other locations. A shower, with its stream of moving water, also produces negative ions.

- **Light a white candle.** This sets a meditative mood and quickly removes unpleasant energy from any surrounding. White contains all colors of the spectrum and creates comfort and calm.

- **Spray rosewater or use other types of aromatherapy.** The delicate scent of rosewater is lovely. I find it effective in soothing an emotional hangover. Inhaling lavender or spearmint essential oil is uplifting too. You can also select an essential oil and put it in a diffuser, which spreads the scent in the air. Try lavender, spearmint, juniper, sage, frankincense, or myrrh. Experience the sublime scent of any of these, as they purify your energy and the room. Stay away from synthetic oils, though, because they contain toxic ingredients.

- **Get out in nature.** Hug a tree. Do some Earthing by putting your bare feet or your entire body on the ground. Rejoice in the flowers. Hold a rock in your hand. Breathe in fresh air to cure an emotional hangover. (Inhaling oxygen is a treatment for alcohol hangovers too.) The purity of nature can restore your clarity and mood.

- **Create a sacred space for meditation.** Place candles, incense, flowers, a statue of Quan Yin, or an image of a sacred teacher on a simple table in a quiet corner. Meditating in sacred space protects and builds positive energy, which is a balm for emotional hangovers.

- **Seek emotional support.** If negative energy is lingering from a toxic interaction, you may need some extra support to release it. Talking out the situation with a friend or therapist will allow you to voice and dispel any remaining negativity. ■

Your goal as an empath is to protect yourself from energy vampires so you can experience maximum wellness. Along with the strategies you now have from this chapter, I strongly recommend that you continue your own emotional healing work. The Law of Attraction states that we attract what we give off, both positive and negative. As a result, we can attract and absorb negative emotions from others that we haven't resolved in ourselves. That's why we are extra sensitive to some people's energy but not others'. The more we heal our fears, anger, and anxieties, the less likely we will be to take these emotions on. As an empath, my emotional healing is a priority. I don't want to be weighed down by other people's issues. The ongoing progress I've made feels truly liberating.

I consider every emotion and every person in our lives, including energy vampires, to be spiritual teachers or "noble adversaries." They teach us to overcome negativity and to heal ourselves. They teach us to set boundaries and to learn to love ourselves more. Of course, no one would wish for toxic relationships. But when we encounter them, let's do everything possible to protect ourselves and to be the bigger person as we learn to forgive the part of others that has forgotten how to love.

EMPATH AFFIRMATION

I will protect my energy around draining people. I will learn how to set healthy boundaries. I will learn to say "no" at the right times. I will listen to my intuition about the relationships that are nurturing for me.

Chapter 6

EMPATHS, PARENTING, AND RAISING SENSITIVE CHILDREN

B eing a parent is one of the most demanding life choices anyone can make, but it's especially challenging for empaths. Our sensitive nervous systems are so easily overwhelmed by the intense increase in sensory input and busyness. Despite this, both my empath patients and friends who are raising children consistently report that they find the rewards far outweigh the stresses of parenthood. They often describe their children as the light of their lives.

Raising children undoubtedly offers great gifts to all parents. Children can bring not only emotional bonding and a sense of family but also wonder, tenderness, and fun. Fathers and mothers who are empaths experience great joy and nurturing in their roles. Parents have the opportunity to get a new human being off to a good start. Empaths are naturally giving; they love to fulfill this role. The guidance they provide their sons and daughters is a sacred contribution to their growth. Children are also powerful teachers who help their parents grow by giving them opportunities to learn patience, limit setting, and love. When empaths have self-care strategies, they become incredible parents because of their compassion, intuition, and ability to support their children's own sensitivities.

But—and this is a big but—along with the countless gifts of parenting, the stressors are ongoing, even when you're fortunate enough to have a supportive mate, family, babysitter, or nanny. Empaths must be aware of these stressors because they are prone to sensory overload. Some of these stressors include less time alone, more socializing, a packed daily schedule with frequent food preparation, dirty diapers, sleep deprivation, the generally high noise level from children crying and screaming—and as kids get older, the many parties, sleepovers, messy rooms, sports teams, and school events. One empath told me, "I love children and helped to raise my beautiful stepchild. It is a precious gift to have a child's soul entrusted to your care. The noise and chaos were hard, but worth it. The biggest sacrifices I had to make were my time and freedom."

In light of all this, when deciding whether to be a parent, it's wise to mindfully weigh the many benefits and stressors. Some empaths decide not to have children because they aren't drawn to the parenting role or know it would be too demanding for their sensitive nature. Others choose to have just one child, and some are happy being doting aunts, uncles, godparents, or mentors, commitments that require less time and energy. These options also provide a sense of family and joy.

PARENTING IS A MINDFUL CHOICE AND A MATTER OF DESTINY

Since empaths are so sensitive, having children must be a mindful choice. I help my patients consider the pros and cons of parenting. This way they won't romanticize the process without grasping the impact on their nervous system, privacy, and sensitivities. Intuition is central to making a good decision. I guide my patients to tune in to whether having children feels right in their gut. Here are two intuitive techniques I suggest for you.

~~~~~~~~~~~~~~~~~

MEDITATION EXERCISE

Technique 1. Tune In to Your Gut

Find a calm and quiet place to connect with your intuition. Then, inwardly pose this question to yourself: "Is it the best choice for me to have a child?" Next, listen to how your inner voice responds.

- An intuitive "yes" can feel comfortable, energizing, excited, balanced, or flowing.

- An intuitive "no" can feel like a sinking or sick feeling, a sense of discomfort or contraction, or like trying to force something or hitting a wall.

Intuition will help you make the best choice. You must have children because you want them and not to please your parents, who may want grandchildren, or because society expects it. Of course there may still be some anxiety about the decision. That's natural. But the basic "intuitive yes" about moving forward must be there. Also, you and your partner must be in sync with this decision. If you're not, seek help from a therapist or guide.

~~~~~~~~~

MEDITATION EXERCISE

Technique 2. Meditate on the Child's Spirit

In a quiet moment, meditate on connecting with the spirit of your child. Empaths can often feel this with their heightened sensitivity. You may intuit a life force approaching, a mutual yearning to meet, or a feeling of happiness. If you experience these intuitions or others that confirm your connection with this soul, that is a strong intuitive "yes" to consider. My patients who are having difficulty conceiving often use this technique to get in touch with their child's spirit and say, "Hello—we want you with all our hearts." This formal introduction and invitation can energetically facilitate conception.

Parenting involves choice, but it's also about karma and destiny. Some people simply aren't meant to have children, which is perfectly fine. Their spiritual lessons will come in other forms that are ideal for them. Sometimes, we are destined to care for a particular child, who may also be meant to help you. This is a powerful impetus for a soul to be born or adopted and creates a strong bond between you. I've worked with couples who end up separating after they have kids, as if the primary purpose of their union was to bring these beings into the world. Also, it may be your destiny to coparent your partner's children. Remember that all these variables factor in when it comes to child-rearing and parenting in your own life.

> THERE REALLY ARE PLACES IN THE HEART YOU DON'T EVEN KNOW EXIST UNTIL YOU LOVE A CHILD.
>
> **Anne Lamott**

COPING SKILLS FOR EMPATHIC PARENTS

All the usual stresses of parenting are amplified if you are an empath. How do you balance work, and your relationships with your partner, kids, family, and friends without freaking out, especially if you're easily overwhelmed? The secret to thriving as an empath parent is to have strategies in place to counter tension and overstimulation. Of course, this is important for all parents, but because empaths have a lower threshold for stress, anxiety, and sensory overload, these tools can make or break their sanity and well-being. Empaths are most comfortable with consistency, so instead of being thrown off-center by the ongoing twists and turns of parenthood, a set of reliable strategies will prepare you to cope in a more constructive way.

Sensitivity is a mixed bag. Although a parent's empathy benefits both kids and parents psychologically, the impact on the parent's physical health is a different story. A recent study in *Health Psychology* reports that empathetic parents experience compromised immunity and low-grade systemic inflammation from having to regularly deal with their children's depression and upsets.[1] It's easy to understand why many physicians recommend stress-reduction techniques such as exercise and meditation to strengthen a parent's immune system.

In the spirit of self-care, naturally empathetic parents and parents who are empaths can practice the following strategies to reduce stress and to stay calm and balanced. They will help mothers and fathers be mindful of how they express their emotions to their kids, while still allowing parents to feel deeply. Empaths get overloaded easily when they do too much without breaks. As parents, they would do well to incorporate these tools and add some breathing room into their days, even for short periods. A little goes a long way in rejuvenating energy and serenity.

Twelve Action Steps for Parents to Achieve Balance and Reduce Sensory Overload

1. **Start the day with a gratefulness affirmation.** This sets a positive and uplifting tone to the day instead of anxiously starting off with endless to-do lists. Whether silently or aloud, begin your day saying, "I am grateful for this day and for my health, my connection to Spirit, and my kids and family. Thank you for all these blessings. May I stay calm. May I stay happy. May I be loving."

2. **Remember to breathe.** Rushing causes us to hold our breath or to breathe shallowly, which traps tension in the body. Throughout your busy day, program yourself to take at least one conscious deep breath periodically to release tension. You might want to set the timer on your phone to remind you.

3. **Create alone time.** To counter the demands of raising children, empaths must schedule at least a few minutes alone each day to recharge. Spend some time in nature if you can or in a sacred space at home. A five-minute timeout in the bathroom or closet (if those are your only places of refuge) may be all you need. If you have a partner who is available, they can watch the kids. Otherwise, you can enjoy time alone when your child is napping, away on a playdate, or maybe at soccer

practice. If it's safe to leave your school-age children alone briefly, close your bedroom door and shut your eyes for the simple pleasure of slowing down.

One friend started a babysitting co-op. She and a neighbor traded taking care of each other's children so that each mom could have a free afternoon once a week.

It's good role modeling to say to your children, "I need some alone time." Since your kids want your attention, they might be momentarily upset, but it nourishes them and you to care for your own energy. You'll be a less irritable parent. One empath mom told me, "The best thing I can give my daughter is me being happy. When I have time to myself, I can be a better mom."

If you're lucky enough to have loved ones who can watch the kids, taking miniretreats away is wonderful. After fourteen years of marriage, one empath and mother of two girls in middle school finally took herself to a hotel for a weekend. "No spiritual conferences to attend," she said, "There was just time to be by myself and write because I had forgotten the sound of my own inner voice."

4. **Listen to soothing music.** Music has the power to heal, inspire, and to transform tension. It is an instant energy shifter. It helps you and your baby as you rock the little one to sleep, and later, it can be a source of calm for everyone in your home. Just hearing a song we love settles an overwrought nervous system. Of course, music is a balm when

you can have those moments alone too. To start
my day, I love listening to "The Great Bell Chant,"
which is narrated by Buddhist monk Thich Nhat
Hanh, as well as devotional music by the artists Enya,
Snatam Kaur, Tina Malia, or Wah!

5. **Meditate.** Finding bits of time to meditate breaks
   the stress cycle and quiets the nervous system. As
   one empath mother told me, "After I meditate, I'm
   calmer. Then I don't get pulled into the drama of my
   son's tantrums." Try using the Three-Minute Heart
   Meditation (see chapter 2) at home when a loved one
   or babysitter can watch the kids. If you're on the run,
   practice the meditation in the car after you drop off
   the kids or even in a public restroom if that is the only
   private space that is available. You may want to get a
   small fountain or some water element at home so that
   the tranquil sound of water flowing can permeate your
   environment and help calm you and your children.

   While meditating, you can concentrate on an
   inspiring image, such as the ocean, the night sky, or
   a forest. You can also try focusing on how much you
   love your kids and what a miracle they are in your life.
   This will ignite your heart energy during times of stress.
   Breathe, center, feel your heart, and reconnect with
   yourself and your higher power as you gently exhale
   accumulated tension. It's incredible how restorative a
   short meditation can be.

6. **Take power naps.** If you have young children, you
   might feel the urge to catch up on laundry while

they're napping, but this is the perfect time for you to take a power nap. Just twenty minutes will revive you and provide an energy boost that will carry you through the rest of your busy day. Empaths are extremely open to receiving healing energy during sleep. The laundry can wait until later.

7. **Set boundaries.** Strive to set clear boundaries and enforce them. There is probably no harder place to set limits than with your children, but it's healthy to say "no" to unreasonable requests and bad behavior. I've seen that it's hard for some of my empath patients to set boundaries. They are overvigilant caretakers, constantly meeting their children's demands, even when they're inappropriate. It's often difficult for empaths to tolerate their children crying because the emotions pierce through their own bodies. However, it's the sign of a capable parent to say, "I know you want to chat with your friends on social media, but you can only go online after you finish your homework." Or maybe the scenario is one like this: "I understand that you want that glazed donut, but it's not healthy for you. If you don't stop crying, we're going to have to leave the store right now." Then be prepared to abandon your shopping cart and exit.

   To become socialized, kids need boundaries. No one ever gets everything they want. Children must learn to deal with frustration; otherwise, they will become demanding and self-centered. When parents set reasonable and clear boundaries and enforce them, the home is much calmer—which also creates a more tranquil environment for empaths. Everyone knows their limits and what's expected of them. Without boundaries, there's chaos.

8. **Don't be a helicopter parent.** Empath parents are highly intuitive and pick up on what their children are feeling and thinking—often to an extreme. As a result, they can become overly anxious, and so they hover and micromanage. This doesn't serve the kids though; it can make them anxious and resentful too. Use your intuition, but be mindful of smothering your children with constant concerns. Letting go more will reduce your stress level.

    Also, beware of invading your children's emotional space when they're upset. It's hard to see your children deal with pain without interfering, but it's important to give them some time to process their feelings. Identify which emotions belong to you and be responsible for them while allowing your children to identify their own feelings. This way, you will also let them work things out in their own way as they learn their own lessons. This doesn't mean that you won't be there to guide them, but it will stop you from smothering them and jumping in too quickly to fix their problems.

9. **Center your own energy.** Your energy affects your children's energy, so being mindful of how you express emotions is stabilizing for your kids. Acting out of frustration when you're in a bad mood will only leave them upset and confused. An empath

mom who is single told me that her kids were
always in afterschool programs because of her heavy
workload. She noticed that whenever she had a bad
day at work, the kids
would start whining and
acting out in the car
as soon as she picked
them up. She gradually
figured out that it was
her energy that was
the source of their
crankiness. They were
absorbing and reacting
to her anxious state. So
she made it a point to stop thinking about work
as soon as she left her job and, instead, plan a fun
evening with the kids. Her children responded well
to this shift. Her gentle and playful energy had a
tranquil affect on them.

> YOUR PRESENCE IS
> THE MOST PRECIOUS
> GIFT YOU CAN GIVE TO
> ANOTHER HUMAN BEING.
> **Marshall B. Rosenberg, PhD**

10. **Watch what you eat.** Empaths are prone to
    hypoglycemia (see chapter 3). We often benefit from
    frequent small protein meals to stay grounded and
    to maintain steady energy. Skipping meals makes us
    more susceptible to exhaustion, anxiety, and sensory
    overload. Avoid sugar binges, which cause mood
    swings and frustrated behavior with your kids and
    partner. Try to eat healthy and clean foods to keep
    you balanced and energized. Minimize your alcohol
    intake too. Some empath parents turn to alcohol or
    other substances such as anti-anxiety medications

(mother's little helper) to make it through a stressful day with their kids. Don't fall into this trap.

11. **Decompress through exercise.** Movement melts stress and relaxes us. It gets our endorphins (the body's natural painkillers) flowing and decreases stress hormones. Yoga, stretching, walking, and hiking are all wonderful ways to reduce stress and sensory overload. If your partner is amenable, try alternating workout nights so that each of you gets an opportunity to exercise.

12. **Have fun with your kids.** Remember what precious beings of light your children are rather than dwelling on annoyances. Focus on the privilege of parenting them. The laughter of happy children is healing. Let your empath self release stress by joining them in their joy.

Throughout the extraordinary experience of child-rearing, remember to be compassionate with yourself. Accept that you can't do everything. Even without children, empaths are overstimulated by too much people contact. As much as you might want to say "yes" to certain social requests, at times it's more self-preserving to decline activities that are not a priority. I've seen empath moms and dads burn out when they didn't say "no." The beauty of parenting is that it can train you to practice self-compassion by expressing your needs, such as, "I need to rest" or "I need take a walk to decompress." When you learn to value self-care, the experience of parenting will be even more magnificent.

RAISING SENSITIVE CHILDREN

Children who are empaths or highly sensitive have nervous systems that react more quickly and strongly to external stimuli. Sometimes they feel too much but don't know how to manage the sensory overload. They see more, hear more, smell more, intuit more, and experience emotions more intensely. For instance, they may not like strong food smells in the kitchen, perfumes, loud talking, or harsh bright lights (particularly fluorescent bulbs). They prefer soft (not scratchy) clothes, beauty, nature, and having one or a few close friends rather than many acquaintances. Our coarse world can assault their sensitivities, and this affects their behavior. Since most sensitive children can't articulate the cause of their upset, enlightened parents need both to help them identify triggers and to offer solutions for their distress (which I'll share below).

Parents need to know what overstimulates their sensitive children. It will mean avoiding some activities. Doing so will calm these children and ward off exhaustion, tantrums, and anxiety. Common triggers include excessive busyness (such as overscheduling their day and leaving no time for breaks), multitasking, no alone time, video games, and watching violent television programs and newscasts, especially at night. Children who experience any of these scenarios might find it harder to fall asleep and require more downtime before bed to unwind. Sensitive children may take longer than other kids to calm down at night because their systems are slower to transition from stimulation to quiet. Also, these children can feel and absorb other people's emotional discomfort, especially from parents and close friends. Because they are "super responders," their hurts cut deep and their joys are extra joyful.

Children who are empaths or have high sensitivity don't have the same mechanisms as other children to screen out light, noise, and the chaos of crowds—for example, the high stimulation of a sports event can feel overwhelming. Cheering, clapping, and booing can feel jarring, even painful, to them. They also don't respond well to loud music, honking, and hammering or noisy power tools. These sounds agitate them, while the peaceful sounds of birds chirping, gentle wind chimes, and water all soothe them. Highly empathic children may cry more and cope by retreating into solitude to self-regulate sensory overload.

Typically, schools and the rest of society don't give these exceptional children much understanding. Conventional physicians and teachers often label them "shy," "antisocial," or "fussy," or else they're diagnosed with social phobia, an anxiety disorder, or depression. Because they may be quieter, more thoughtful, deep, and gentle, rather than extremely verbal or assertive, others can perceive them as withdrawn. In view of these misconceptions, the parent's role is critical in supporting their sensitivities, intuition, creativity, wisdom, and in teaching them tools to cope with the world.

As a child who was an empath, I received no support from my physician parents for my sensitivities. It wasn't because they didn't love me. They simply didn't know what an empath was or how to understand my special needs. They wanted me to be happy, but they didn't think encouraging my sensitivities would lead me there. They called me "overly sensitive" and said that I needed a "thicker skin." These well-intended comments made me believe there was something wrong with me. Because I felt misunderstood and invisible as an empath child, I have become especially passionate about educating parents about their sensitive children.

Knowing that your child is an empath or highly sensitive is the first step toward bringing out the best in them. Then you can support their sensitivities as an expression of their excellence, compassion, and depth. To determine if your child is an empath, take the following assessment.

SELF-ASSESSMENT **Is Your Child an Empath?**

- Does your child feel things deeply?
- Do people, crowds, noise, or stress overstimulate your child?
- Does your child have strong reactions to sad or frightening scenes in books or movies?
- Does your child want to escape and hide from family gatherings because there's too much going on?
- Does your child feel different from other kids or complain about not fitting in?
- Is your child a good listener and compassionate?
- Does your child surprise you with intuitive comments about others or yourself?
- Does your child have a strong connection to nature, to plants and animals, or even stuffed animals?
- Does your child require a lot of time alone rather than playing with other kids?
- Does your child take on a friend's stress or upset?
- Does your child take on your own or other people's emotions or stress—and act out when you're angry, upset, or depressed?

- Does your child have one best friend or a few good friends rather than a large social network?

Here's how to score this assessment:

- Nine to twelve yeses indicate a child with extremely strong empath traits.

- Six to eight yeses indicate strong empath traits.

- Four to seven yeses indicate moderate empath traits.

- One to three yeses indicate some empath traits.

- Zero yeses indicate a child who is not an empath.

No matter where your child is on this spectrum, all children can benefit from being taught to honor their particular sensitivities.

THE NEW GENERATION OF INDIGO CHILDREN

In the last decade, much has been said about "Indigo Children," who I believe are a type of empath with strikingly developed intuitive abilities and insight into people and world situations. They are the opposite of the self-absorbed, instant-gratification generation that have a large presence in our culture today. Indigos are a great new wave of children with more awakened intuition, sensitivities, clarity of purpose, and interest in changing the planet for the good. They're often described as "old souls" who have a profound grasp of the human condition. Some say they have lived many lifetimes to attain that knowledge.

A patient described her seventeen-year-old daughter, Anna, as an indigo child. She told me that Anna had prophetic dreams, drew angels in her coloring book since she was very young, and saw spirit visitors in their home. She could also read people intuitively and knew what they were feeling. At seventeen, Anna wants to go into a profession that will help stop global warming, a phenomenon that hurts her soul because, as she says, "I feel the pain of how climate change is threatening our earth."

Indigo children have unique needs that require parents and teachers to become aware of how they treat them. Being sensitive to their gifts will help these children avoid frustration and achieve balance in their lives. Indigo children bring the promise of a higher collective consciousness and a new way of perceiving what happens politically, socially, and economically. As empaths, they bring the possibility for a world with more mutual understanding and harmony in both our personal and global relationships. If you have such an exceptional child, nurture their unique gifts.

SPECIAL CHALLENGES FOR SENSITIVE BOYS

Boys who are empaths sometimes have it harder than girls because of shaming cultural stereotypes, such as "boys don't cry." Sensitive boys are often humiliated for their gentleness and compassion and are told to "man up." They grow up ashamed of who they are. They may cry more as children to cope with being overwhelmed or when they sense other people's pain. Sometimes they shed tears of joy when they're happy or are touched by the tenderness of life. They tend to dislike the adrenaline rush and noise of violent action films or video games, and they avoid heavy contact sports like football or boxing where risk and potential injury are involved. As a result, they might not be invited to participate in many activities with their friends.

Sensitive boys are hurt by this rejection and feel as if they don't fit in. In Western culture boys are often reinforced for risky behavior, but boys who are empaths aren't usually risk takers. They prefer safer and more predictable outcomes. Since they're intuitively aware of danger signals, they may be more cautious, which can be misinterpreted as being a "wimp."

Parents with sensitive sons need to help them accept their gifts of sensitivity, while keeping the cultural stereotypes associated with gentleness in men in perspective. For instance, sensitive men may be viewed as feminine, "too soft," or "unmanly." In the old John Wayne, tough-guy paradigm of masculinity, men are strong and silent, and they don't express pain, fear, or tears, lest they be considered weak. In the new enlightened paradigm, men are considered strong when they can be vulnerable, gentle, and secure enough to show tears. This doesn't mean that they are overfeminized but that they have learned to embrace both their masculine and feminine sides to become a whole person. I urge you to talk with your son about the positive aspects of being sensitive—how he's thoughtful, smart, caring, creative, intuitive, and attuned to people and nature. When your son knows you support him, it builds his self-esteem.

Sadly, some sensitive boys rebel by trying to be someone they are not, or they get involved with alcohol or other addictions to numb their intense empathy so they can fit in with their peers. They may become angry at being shamed, rejected, or bullied by other boys and act out at home or at school. One mother told me, "My sensitive son was bullied at school. He broke down, saying he doesn't trust people. He's afraid to leave the house because of the bullying. He doesn't want to get hurt again." It's important to discuss bullying with your son by validating his feelings. Tell him that he isn't to blame. The bully is the one with emotional problems, not him. Never tolerate anyone shaming your son when he expresses sensitive behavior. Stand up for him. Involve the school authorities, and send the message that there is zero tolerance for bullying.

Sensitive fathers are fantastic role models for their sons. Fathers who are proud to be loving and sensitive, even if they're not empaths, send the right message to their boys. Good fathers are strong and sensitive men, who have good hearts and aren't afraid to express their feelings to their families. As a parent, your role modeling goes a long way by showing your son how to be a well-balanced man and lead a loving life.

HOW TO SUPPORT SENSITIVE CHILDREN

The Magic and Stress of Pregnancy and Infancy

What possible factors contribute to children becoming empaths? Some may begin as empaths in utero, able to intensely feel everything, both joyful and stressful. These children are born with high sensitivities, emerging from the womb extremely responsive to external stimuli, even more so than other infants. In these instances, it seems that the empath trait is passed on genetically.[2] Sometimes, though, this temperament emerges as a result of early childrearing. Parental role-modeling is important. Children learn from their parents' empath traits.[3]

Supporting an empath child begins in pregnancy. Everything that happens during this period affects the growing fetus. In fact, whether or not a child turns out to be an empath, it's well known that fetuses are sensitive to the emotional environment of their parents. It has been shown, for instance, that some fetuses enjoy Mozart but are agitated by rap music.[4]

Playing relaxing music during pregnancy can help calm you and your baby.

A mother's stress level matters too. Research has shown that maternal stress hormones cross the placenta and circulate in the fetus, increasing a child's tendency to be "highly strung."[5] When a mother experiences ongoing conflict with her partner or others, the fetus gears itself up to deal with this kind of high-pressure environment and may then be predisposed to other stress-related symptoms after birth.

The neurological wiring for sensitivity develops in the womb. It's important to surround a pregnant mother with as much serenity as possible. Then both mom and fetus will be bathed in endorphins, the body's "bliss" neurochemicals and natural painkillers. Meditation, laughter, exercise, and being in nature all boost endorphin levels. I recommend that mothers use the following meditation daily during and after pregnancy to reap the serene spiritual, emotional, and physical benefits of endorphins.

PROTECTION STRATEGY
A Meditation for Mothers:
Feeling the Goddess Within

Take five minutes to breathe slowly and deeply. Put your hand on your heart and flood yourself with love and appreciation for who you are as a mother. Experience the blessing, the gratitude, the warmth, and the connection of being a parent. Mothers are goddesses of creation. Maternal nurturing is an act of deep love. Feel the power of the mother goddess deep within you. She is the part of you that is connected to the earth and all natural cycles in a profoundly mystical way. The mother goddess was worshipped by various cultures in ancient times. Exalt in the mother goddess within you. Feel her primal power, and hail her presence in your being. ■

Your fetus reacts as you react, so having a positive state of mind is important. Keep your baby calm by being calm yourself. Think optimistic and peaceful thoughts. Also, move your body with mindfulness and ease. The gentle swaying your fetus experiences when you take a slow walk puts you both in a restful state, Also, after birth, rocking motions help your baby to sleep.

Empath mothers must be kind to themselves during pregnancy since feeling a new being inside can heighten their sensitivities. To attune to your baby, place your hand over your belly, lovingly stroke it, and send your child heart energy. Your partner can do this with you too. It's a way of energetically saying "hi" and establishing a sweet bond between parents and child. Any anxiety you might have felt about being pregnant can dissipate when you intuitively tune in. One empath mom shared this with me: "I could feel the growing fetus. My daughter stretched out her wings in all corners of my belly like a butterfly. I knew everything was okay."

Empath fathers must adjust to a new level of sensitivity during the pregnancy too. One father who is a physical empath told me he experienced his wife's morning sickness, even before she was aware of it. On an unconscious level, he intuitively merged with her body and felt her sensations. He was better able to draw a boundary between his wife's energy and his own after learning meditation and grounding exercises in our sessions. Using these strategies, he was then less prone to take on her symptoms.

Once your baby is born, if you suspect your child is an empath, take extra care to create a pleasing and peaceful environment, with soft lighting and minimal noise. Breastfeeding will deepen your bonding, as well as carrying your baby in a sling, which allows both of you to feel the closeness of your energies. This is so much more nurturing than putting a baby in a crib with a pacifier or a bottle whenever they cry.

The Effect of Early Trauma on an Adult's Sensitivity

As a psychiatrist, I've observed how childhood neglect or mistreatment can affect the sensitivity level of adults. As I discussed in chapter 1, a number of empaths I've worked with have experienced early childhood emotional or physical trauma, which wore down their defenses and made them more sensitive throughout their lives.

An angry environment can especially impact a sensitive child. Recently, researchers at the University of Oregon found that infants become agitated around argumentative and angry voices and that ongoing exposure to arguments can make them more reactive to other kinds of stress and sleep disturbances.[6] Parents must realize the effect of anger and yelling on their baby. They must learn to calm themselves and address anger in healthier ways. Infants are totally dependent. They can't walk away from your anger and must suffer the toxic consequences. The study also revealed that dire stressors of abuse and mistreatment can significantly alter a baby's brain development—a sobering eye-opener.

I recommend that all empaths who have experienced neglectful or abusive parenting get help from a therapist or other qualified guide to heal these wounds. I also suggest repeating a variation of the Serenity Prayer (top of the next page) to release

the past, as well as any expectation that your parents will change.
Saying this prayer can protect you
from harboring toxic resentments
and pain from your upbringing.
It will help you find acceptance
as well as more peace and humor,
no matter how limited your par-

> PLEASE GRANT ME THE
> SERENITY TO ACCEPT
> THE PARENTS THAT I
> CANNOT CHANGE.
>
> **The Serenity Prayer (variation)**

ents were. The fewer resentments we hold, especially about our
family, the better it is for us and our own children.

In addition, it's also healing and important to forgive yourself for your own mistakes as a parent with your kids and
family. Don't beat yourself up. It's impossible to be perfect,
though it's a good practice to quickly make amends to your
loved ones when you've been, say, impatient, frustrated, or
irritable. As you make amends,
I suggest that you lovingly look
at your children or partner and
repeat the tender traditional
Hawaiian Hoʻoponopono prayer
(to the right).

> I'M SORRY.
> I FORGIVE YOU.
> I LOVE YOU.
> THANK YOU.
>
> **Hoʻoponopono prayer**

Saying this prayer creates positive energy while it clears out
resentment and hurt feelings. It
reinforces the great spiritual lessons of parenting, which include
self-love, humility, and the commitment to honor your own,
your children's, and your partner's sensitivities.

Twenty Tips for Nurturing Empathic Children

It's wonderful to support sensitive children and embrace their abilities. This will make all the difference in their feeling comfortable in their own skin now and as they mature into sensitive adults. The following strategies can help you and them:

1. **Encourage your child's sensitivities and intuition.**
   Invite your child to speak openly about their abilities to you and to others who are supportive. Make it clear to them that not everyone is accepting of these gifts and identify people who might be safe. You can also share some of your empathic experiences, such as the tendency to take on others' emotions and stress, although I wouldn't overshare painful details. The point is to be there for your child, not therapy for yourself. Teach your child to value their uniqueness and to trust their gut feelings and inner voice. Then they will see their gifts as natural. These conversations will help your child feel seen and better understand their own reactions.

2. **Honor your child's feelings.** Listen carefully to what your child feels, and respect their feelings. This may mean allowing them the occasional day off from school to wind down or letting them play alone more often. You don't want to indulge isolation, but you do want to support the needed time alone that is critical for an empath child's well-being. If your child needs to crawl under the dining room table or leave a large gathering, don't drag them back into the party. Don't shame them for wanting

to escape. Just let them stay on the sidelines where they can observe and absorb without becoming overwhelmed. They are participating, but in their own way. You may be surprised at the insights they share after the crowd disperses.

3. **Educate family members and teachers about your empath child.** Do not allow others to judge or criticize your child, such as telling them that they need to "toughen up" because they become easily hurt or upset. Family members and others may not mean to be disrespectful. They just need to understand more about your child's sensitive temperament. Because the school environment can be harsh and unsupportive of empaths, educate your child's teachers about their gifts and their tendency for sensory overload. Also, ask them to support your child if they are being bullied or teased at school.

4. **Trust your intuition.** Keep tuning in to your own intuition about what your child needs. Don't second-guess your inner voice or let others talk you out of what it is telling you. Let your intuition guide you in raising your child.

5. **Help your child recognize when they've absorbed other people's emotions.** Explain to your son or daughter that sensitive children can easily be affected by the emotions of the people around them, perhaps more so than other kids. You might tell them it's like being able to feel a raincloud or sunshine above

someone's head that nobody else can see. You can show them a picture of Joe Btfsplk, the famous comic-strip character in *Li'l Abner,* who always has a dark cloud hovering over him. He means well but brings misfortune to those around him.

Empath children can sense the positive and negative vibes that people emit. So when you notice a sudden and unexplainable shift in your child's mood or energy level, tell them it's likely they're picking up another person's emotions. If the experience feels good, that's fine, of course, but if it's uncomfortable or tiring, support your child in getting some distance and talk to them about the experience. Once your child learns to distinguish which emotions are theirs and which belong to another, they will be less confused.

6. **Be an emotional stabilizer.** Empath children tend to take on their parents' anxiety and want to make things better for them. Try to stay steady in your emotions and avoid expressing excessive anxiety around them. One mother told me, "If I'm anxious, my sensitive son feels it, which destabilizes him and triggers tantrums. My goal is to stay centered. When I'm centered, it makes him feel secure." Be aware that highly empathic children can mirror your emotions and symptoms—and that empath parents can do the same with their kids.

7. **Don't argue in front of your child or anywhere they can overhear.** Sensitive children feel it is their

job to help their parents get along better. They become more frightened and absorb more anger than children who are not empaths do. Anxiety and arguments overstimulate them. If you must argue with your partner or others, do so when your kids can't hear. Like highly sensitive adults, highly sensitive children can be wounded by yelling. They may believe they are to blame for the conflict. They also absorb the negativity and want to fix the problem, which is an inappropriate role for them.

8. **Encourage your child to take time alone to be quiet and creative.** Empath children thrive on free and unstructured time. It's an opportunity for them to be creative and allow their imaginations to wander. They recharge and calm down when they are alone, which reduces their stimulation threshold. Support your child in having these magical quiet interludes to replenish. You can do this by not overscheduling your child and by giving them permission to have regular timeouts, especially when they're cranky, whiny, or overwhelmed.

9. **Teach your child breathing and meditation exercises.** When sensitive children are stressed or feel as if they've taken on other people's emotions (including your own), it's important that they learn to take a few deep breaths to calm down. In addition, they can close their eyes for a couple of minutes and visualize a relaxing image, such as the ocean, an adorable pet, or a happy day at the park. Ask

them to focus on this image as they breathe out all discomfort and inhale calm and happiness. This will teach them how to break the cycle of sensory overload and re-center themselves.

10. **Encourage your child to express their dreams.** Empath children often love to share their night dreams. Create a breakfast ritual where they can talk about them in detail. Discuss how the dream made them feel, what emotions came up, and what message they think the dream was communicating. For instance, if your child is frustrated in a dream, try to identify a source of the frustration in daily life too so that it can be relieved. You might suggest that they keep a dream journal in which they record their dreams each night. They can also draw or paint images from their dreams in the journal.

11. **Help your child practice shielding around energy vampires.** Encourage your child to recognize draining and upsetting people and to set healthy boundaries with them, whether these people are adults or other kids. For instance, your child can limit the time they spend with a drainer by saying, "I have to go meet my mom now," and they can simply stay away from angry people to prevent getting dumped on. If they can't avoid the person, teach your child to visualize a protective shield of white light a few inches away from their skin that completely surrounds their body from head to toe. Explain that this shield will repel negative energy so that they don't take on

uncomfortable feelings, while the shield will also allow positive energy to come through.

12. **Ground your child with drumming.** Drumming is a primal sound that can calm children. When your sensitive child gets overstimulated or cranky, have fun together beating on a drum in a slow and steady rhythm that mimics the heart rate. Shaking a rattle can also help relieve pressure. When your child is older, you can join a drumming circle with your community—as long as the group isn't too large.

13. **Reduce exposure to stimulating situations.** Because empath children can become irritable from too much sensory input, limit your child's time in highly stimulating environments, such as Disneyland and other amusement parks. Two to three hours may be the maximum time for them, although others in your party can tolerate more. It's no fun dragging around a screaming child when you're at "the happiest place on earth." So go early, when the crowds are thinner. Then take a break when you see signs of overload and return to your hotel or home. You can always go back for more later, after everyone has had a chance to refresh and re-center themselves.

14. **Create downtime before your child goes to sleep.** This means no TV, cell phones, social media, video games, computers, or other electronic devices before bed. It often takes an empath child longer to wind down at night. Darkness and quiet

decrease stimulation, which allows children to rest more effectively. Singing lullabies soothes them to sleep as well.

15. **Limit your child's intake of processed food, carbohydrates, and sugar.** This will lower your child's stimulation level by preventing the mood swings from sugar highs as well as carbohydrate cravings and rushes. Processed foods are full of chemicals and stripped of nutrients, which also makes them less digestible. They can cause your kids to be irritable, have too much or too little energy, and blur their focus. Sensitive children are sensitive to foods. Educate them about how what they eat influences their mood and energy level.

16. **Intervene before tantrums.** If your child is upset or on the verge of a tantrum, dim the lights to soften the environment and turn on relaxing music—no hard rock, heavy metal, or rap. Sometimes it's helpful to play nature sounds, such as flowing water. Also ask your child to slow down and take some long, deep breaths. Teach them to exhale stress and to inhale peacefulness.

17. **Use aromatherapy with essential oils (no synthetics).** Lavender is relaxing. Rub one to two drops on your child's third eye (in the center of the forehead), or heat lavender oil so that the scent permeates the room (you can usually get the device that safely heats essential oils wherever you purchase the oil). Taking

a warm bath at bedtime with a few drops of lavender, chamomile, sandalwood, or ylang ylang oil in the water can be calming. Tell your child to imagine washing away all stress in the bath. Adding a half a cup of Epsom salts is useful for removing toxins and relieving stress as well. A massage during or after the evening bath can soothe your child and encourage sleep too.

18. **Use pet therapy.** Pets are grounding and offer children unconditional love. They are good companions and can quiet an upset child. Empath children have a special affinity for animals and may be able to communicate with them on deep levels if they are animal empaths. Dogs can be effective in settling down overactive or aggressive kids.

19. **Use gemstones.** Try giving your child a quartz or pink or black tourmaline crystal to hold. These can feel secure in the hand, while they subtly are grounding and calming.

20. **Help your child turn the dial down on stress.** Along with the above tips, you can also teach your child to use the following visualization to quiet down and break the stress cycle whenever they're feeling overloaded. They can use it at home, at school, or with their friends. This technique is a part of the basic tool kit for all sensitive children.

PROTECTION STRATEGY
FOR SENSITIVE CHILDREN
Turn the Dial Down on Stress

When your child feels overstimulated, here's what you can say to them: In your imagination, picture a big dial on a table in front of you. It has numbers on it, and they go from 10 on the left side to zero on the right side. Currently, this dial is set at ten. See yourself slowly turning the setting on the dial down, starting with 10. Turn the dial clockwise to the right, as the numbers get smaller and smaller, until you reach zero: 10, 9, 8, 7, 6, 5, 4, 3, 2, and 1. As you turn the dial this way, feel yourself getting more and more relaxed. You are lowering your stress and discomfort. When you reach zero, you will feel calm and happy.

If your child is too young to imagine this dial, you can draw a picture of it and have them point to their stress level. Then slowly count down with them until you reach zero. ■

The practical strategies I present in this chapter will make raising an empathic child a calmer and more joyful experience for your whole family. It is a blessing to support the special gifts of empath children. When they learn to manage their sensitivities early on, their childhood and adult lives will be easier and more fulfilling. From this perspective, we're reminded that parenting is a sacred responsibility.

THE FUTURE OF ENLIGHTENED PARENTING

My dream is that education about what it means to be an empathic child begins at the earliest stages for parents, as well as for educators in our schools. Instead of shaming children for their sensitivities, parents, teachers, and authority figures can support these abilities and help empathic children and their loved ones understand them. In this way, children will learn to understand and cope with their sensitivities as well, which can ignite their creativity and confidence.

Together we can begin to embrace sensitive children and adults. The world would be more harmonious and peaceful if our leaders were highly sensitive people with big, strong hearts. Through my workshops, books, online courses, and audio programs, I have dedicated my career to educating as many people as I can—including leaders in all fields and businesses, as well as healers and parents—about empaths and parenting sensitive children. Imagine the glorious day when all of us can be open to the wonders of the sensitivities in our children and ourselves.

EMPATH AFFIRMATION

For children and parents to use:
I will embrace my sensitivities
and take time to rest and recharge.
I will express my needs with supportive
people. I will not hide my gifts.
I will be authentic. I will stand
in my power. I am proud to
be a sensitive and
loving person.

Chapter 7

EMPATHS AND WORK

E mpaths must be comfortable in their work environment to feel healthy and happy, as is true for most people. However, since empaths may be less defended against stress than others, it's harder for them to bounce back without becoming exhausted or ill from their jobs. Empaths are creators, inventors, visionaries, artists, and people who feel first. We see the big picture while navigating the workday. We often think out of the box, which may make corporate or traditional office settings too restrictive, but when our talents are tapped, work can be fulfilling, energizing, and fun.

Empaths thrive in the right work environment. A job that suits our temperament can inspire us, put us in a creative zone, and boost our vitality and passion. Also knowing that we've contributed to the greater good, even in the smallest way, satisfies an empath's giving heart. The wrong job, however, can suck the life right out of us and trigger a cascade of emotional and physical symptoms in response to stress and emotional overload. In this chapter, I will share some secrets to finding the best career to support your gifts and sensory needs. Since we're typically at work for many hours, it's crucial for an empath's well-being to feel at ease there most of the time.

THRIVING IN THE WORK ENVIRONMENT

Three major factors play a role in our comfort level: the meaning we get from our work, the energy of the people around us, and the energy of the physical space. See where you currently stand with these factors, and begin to envision how you might improve your situation.

1. Meaningful work

Empaths enjoy doing meaningful work that is in sync with their sensitivities. We like to feel that we've made a difference in people's lives or to the world. Such work can be anything from gardening, to running a catering business, to working in the helping professions. Most importantly, the situation must intuitively feel right in our body and not sap our energy, though of course some days can be draining in any job.

> HAVE THE COURAGE TO FOLLOW YOUR HEART AND INTUITION. THEY SOMEHOW ALREADY KNOW WHAT YOU TRULY WANT TO BECOME.
>
> Steve Jobs

I feel blessed to have found work I'm passionate about as a writer, a speaker, and a physician. Like many empaths, I love being of service to others and tapping my creativity. Whether we are healthcare professionals, food servers, attorneys, or hair stylists, we can always be of service to our workmates as well as to others. This is a beautiful mind-set that brings meaning to every line of work. As the poet Rumi says, "Let the beauty we love be what we do. There are hundreds of ways to kneel and kiss the ground." An emphasis on humility and serving others or the greater good can also take the sting out of a stressful or boring job.

The values of love and service can also clarify the priorities for anyone who wants to seek more meaningful work elsewhere. Along with this, focusing on what we can be grateful for in every job, instead of telling ourselves stories about how we dislike it, will set a tone for constructive change, whether or not we stay in that position. Later in this chapter, we will identify the kinds of jobs empaths do and don't function well in. Then you will have more information to help you make the best choice for yourself.

2. The energy of the people around us

Our colleagues, coworkers, and bosses can make or break our comfort level in a job. Sensitive people have a lower threshold for noise, conflict, and office politics. The drama at work that might simply disturb someone else can drain empaths and make us anxious. Sensitive people do better in supportive and friendly settings that value goodwill and collaboration. A high-adrenaline competitive job on Wall Street is not a good match for a sensitive person. Ideally, we want to feel we fit in with our coworkers and supervisors—although the workplace that understands empaths is indeed special. Finding individual coworkers whom empaths can relate to is a more realistic goal. Although not everyone in a workplace is likely to have a positive attitude, much less honor our needs, we're better off when we gravitate to those earth angels who do. Supportive relationships can save us during times of stress and overwhelm.

Still, energy vampires operate all around us. As I discussed in chapter 5, these vampires include narcissists, rageaholics, victims, passive-aggressives, chronic talkers, and drama queens and kings. Any workplace can have such vampires, and being sapped by one takes a physical and emotional toll that affects our job performance. Toxic colleagues, coworkers, and supervisors can be so destructive at work because it's hard to escape them. Empaths can develop health issues—such as fatigue, irritability, pain, or an aggravation of symptoms we already have—when we start to take on someone's negativity.

To be prepared for draining people in the workplace, keep in mind the various strategies we've already discussed to cope with them. One empath told me, "I survive by just doing my job and walking away from anyone who wants a pity party or drama or who is a backstabber or a complainer." An empath nurse shared this about her job: "I work the night shift to avoid the daily gossip, empty small talk, and politics. At night, I can fully devote myself to my patients and the job I love." I also suggest you review chapter 5 and apply its protection strategies—such as setting boundaries, shielding, and meditation—to take good care of yourself in the workplace. With these tools, you can minimize energy depletion. It's also wise to spend time with positive coworkers who can buffer you from the more toxic ones.

3. The energy of the physical space

Every building, office, and stairwell has a subtle energy of its own. Some spaces feel uplifting, while others don't. Empaths can intuit the energy of a physical space with their finely developed sensitivities. I suggest that you tune in to the energy of your workplace to make sure it feels right. Sometimes there is leftover energy, negative or positive, from previous occupants. If you find the energy feels off, you can purify it by spraying rose water in the room. Be mindful that burning sage, though a good space-clearing technique, might set off smoke alarms or disturb coworkers who don't know about energetic cleansing rituals and might be uncomfortable with them. Also, you can meditate alone or with like-minded coworkers in the workplace to infuse it with heart energy and remove any negativity or stagnation. In addition, you might even enlist the help of a feng shui expert, someone who specializes in creating a harmonious environment through the placement of furniture, plants, mirrors, and objects.

Empaths also react to other factors that contribute to how a physical space feels. These include the quality of light, noise and activity levels, smells, air flow, physical proximity to coworkers, and lack of privacy. Empaths don't do well without windows or with harsh fluorescent bulbs. Also, we tend to be a lot or a little claustrophobic, preferring a large perimeter of personal space around us to keep other people's stress at a distance. A cluttered environment can be agitating and depleting, whereas a quiet, spacious, and orderly space will be centering.

Many electronic devices in close proximity can be draining too. Some empaths whom I call "electro-sensitives" are particularly susceptible to this. Electromagnetic radiation from cell phones and computers affect the electromagnetic fields around our brains and hearts. A recent study by the National Toxicology Program ties cellphone radiation to brain and heart tumors in rats.[1] One empath told me, "I cover the monitor as often as possible when I'm at my desk. The bigger monitors are worse. I try not to spend too much time on the computer without breaks, and I limit my cellphone use."

Finally, the energy of the people in a workplace strongly affects how a setting feels. Negative people generate negative energy, and positive people generate positive energy. However, even in a chaotic or anxiety-provoking space, you can create a bubble of serenity around your workstation with flowers, crystals, and sacred objects.

EMOTIONAL CONTAGION AT WORK

Empaths suffer at work when they absorb the stress in their environment. Research has documented that we can catch each other's emotions, a phenomenon known as emotional contagion.[2] One employee's anxiety and panic can spread like a virus in a flash throughout an entire office, lowering morale and productivity. Happiness can also spread throughout a workplace. This positive emotional contagion results in improved cooperation, satisfaction, and performance among coworkers. Although everyone is susceptible to emotional contagion, it is amplified in empaths. The good news is that we can benefit from all the positive energy that circulates at work, and the bad news is that we can pick up coworkers' emotions and illnesses until we learn how not to take them on.

To make matters worse for empaths, many offices today are designed as open space, where desks are not separated from each other by walls or consist of cubicles with only glass partitions. Everyone basically shares the same area. You can hear people talking, complaining, gossiping, coughing, blowing their noses, laughing, humming, cracking their gum, and opening candy wrappers. Also, you can smell your neighbor's perfume or what they're eating and see people walking back and forth. All this means nonstop sensory stimulation. This lack of privacy makes empaths more vulnerable to their coworkers' stress.

Fortunately, there are creative solutions to prevent emotional contagion at work. Shopify, an e-commerce business, surveyed their employees and found that they had a balance of introverts and extroverts. So their office designers modified their offices for both groups. Some sections were noisier and more interactive, whereas other spaces had high-backed couches that could be rolled into a corner for privacy. There were also specific rooms resembling cozy libraries for "quiet work." These design elements offered introverts more space and peace at work, and as a result, they weren't as vulnerable to their coworkers' stress.

Emotional contagion can happen at a distance for empaths too. We can experience it with customers and clients over the phone and actually sense in our body what the person in another setting is feeling. One empathic workshop participant said, "I started a new job selling life insurance. I became anxious making calls, even when customers requested information. My heart went out to families who had no coverage and lost their homes and also to others whose spouses had died unexpectedly. I started taking on their pain!"

Here are some tips for protecting your energy in an overstimulating, emotionally demanding, or crowded environment.

PROTECTION STRATEGY
Set Energetic Boundaries at Work

If you are in an open space or chaotic office, surround the outer edge of your desk with plants or family or pet photos to create a psychological barrier. Sacred objects such as a statue of Quan Yin, St. Francis, or the Buddha, sacred beads, crystals, or protective stones can set an energetic boundary too. It's also important to take bathroom breaks for relief or to walk outside in the fresh air if possible. Noise-canceling earbuds or headphones are useful to muffle conversations and unwelcome sounds. In addition, you can visualize a luminous golden egg surrounding your workstation to repel negativity and admit only positive energy. Visualize yourself as safe and protected within this golden egg. All of these strategies create a cocoon of protection you can rely on. ■

Although you can't control everything in your workplace environment, you do have the power to shift the energy in your immediate vicinity. If you focus on the safe space you create rather than surrounding noise and confusion, you can minimize emotional contagion. Then your work experience will feel much more protected and pleasant.

FINDING THE RIGHT WORK

Some jobs are more satisfying and less stressful for empaths than others. For us to excel and enjoy our work, we want to make the most of our sensitivities, intuition, thoughtfulness, quietness, and creativity—and we don't want to try to be someone we're not.

The Best Jobs for Empaths

I am often asked which careers and working conditions are ideal for empaths. Traditionally, they do better in low-stress jobs with smaller companies or on their own. Empaths are usually happier working at home, away from the office frenzy. Emotional vampires are much easier to deal with by email, phone, and text when they are farther away. If you work from home, you can plan your schedule and regular breaks to decompress.

Many of my empath patients prefer being self-employed because they avoid the drain and overwhelm of coworkers, bosses, and packed schedules. Empaths tend to do better managing their own time rather than having to attend the frequent team meetings that large businesses require (unless the team is positive and cohesive). One empath told me, "I started a home business after many failed attempts at trying to function in offices. I feel much more energized and happier being my own boss." Another empath shared with me, "I'm a seamstress working from home. I could never be in an office forty hours a week. The smells, sounds, and lights make me ill."

If you're employed by a business, it may be feasible to arrange a part-time home office situation and do your work virtually, with ongoing access to the Internet, emails, texts, and Skype. Increasingly, people don't always have to be tied to their office to do their job well, a perk for empaths that allows them to have more choice in their work location. One empath who set up a location-independent business offers this advice to sensitive people: "I used to work for a corporation and was drained by office politics. Now I work by Skype, and it's fantastic. Think about what you love to do and where your skill set is. Then see if you can find a way to share this via the Internet. It's the way the new workplace is going."

However, whether you work at home or alone in an office, be careful not to become isolated or to push yourself too hard. Balance your alone time with people time among colleagues and friends. Some of my empath patients have found that working part-time from home is ideal. You can break up the isolation by scheduling outside meetings. An empath financial advisor who does this said, "I like working independently and meeting one to one with clients in different places. I'm not stuck in an office or at home, and I can arrange my own schedule." All these options may be preferable to the sensory overload of driving to work in heavy traffic or staying in an office eight or more hours a day. Time management is key.

How do these considerations translate into real-world jobs? Empaths do well being self-employed business owners, writers, editors, artists, and in other creative professions. Many actors and musicians, such as Claire Danes, Alanis Morissette,

Scarlett Johansson, and Jim Carrey, have admitted that they are "highly sensitive."

Other good jobs include website and graphic designers, virtual assistants, accountants or lawyers with home offices, and independent electricians, contractors, and plumbers who can set their own appointments. Being a real estate agent or a roving business consultant can be fine too, as long as you establish good boundaries about when you can be reached and you don't over-schedule yourself. Landscape design and gardening, forestry, or other employment that puts you in nature is wonderful for empaths, as are jobs preserving the earth and her ecosystems.

> BEING A SENSITIVE EMPATH IS A BEAUTIFUL THING AS AN ARTIST.
>
> **Alanis Morissette**

Many empaths also go into the helping professions because of their big hearts and desire to serve others. They become physicians, nurses, dentists, physical therapists, psychotherapists, social workers, teachers, yoga instructors, Chinese medical practitioners, massage therapists, clergy, hospice workers, life coaches, and employees or volunteers for non-profit organizations, among other heartfelt jobs. Working with animals, animal rescue, and veterinary medicine are gratifying choices too. But to thrive, empaths in the helping professions must learn how not to take on the symptoms and stress of their patients and clients, a skill I'll discuss later in this chapter. Occupations such as a police officer or firefighter, though heroic, may be too stressful for an empath because of the high sensory stimulation and ongoing physical and emotional trauma inherent in these roles.

Empaths can excel when they use their intuition and compassion to contribute to the well-being of others. One empath patient told me, "I'm a good college professor because I can feel when a student needs extra help." Another empath said, "I am an effective administrator because people are comfortable coming to me. They know I will understand them." Although empaths receive great satisfaction from helping others, we tend to overgive, which puts us at risk for burnout. Even so, when empaths in the helping professions practice self-care strategies, they can have gratifying careers that improve the lives of many.

Empaths are valuable in a host of careers. However, you need to find the right work that supports your skills, gifts, and temperament. An empath's attributes may not be as appreciated in places such as corporations, academia, professional sports, the military, or government. A better match may be the helping professions, the arts, and organizations with more humanistic awareness. So, use your intuition to sense if you are a good fit with the mission and shared goals of an enterprise, its people, and the space and energy of the environment. Just because a job looks good on paper doesn't mean it's right for you. It has to feel right in your gut and your body too.

Jobs for Empaths to Avoid

One of the best ways to take care of your energy is to choose work that enhances your unique empathic gifts and to avoid draining jobs. What jobs are best to steer clear of? Sales is high on that list. Not many empaths enjoy being salespeople, especially if they're introverted. Dealing with the public takes too much out of them. One of my workshop participants who worked in technical support said, "I was too sensitive to constantly deal with angry customers, even if they were right." Like many sensitive people, she picked up people's anger and stress, which felt overwhelming. Another empath told me, "Being a cashier at Walmart nearly gave me an anxiety attack. The crowds, the noise of people talking, the loudspeakers, bright lights, and long hours were exhausting." Whether it's selling cars, diamond rings, or advertising, empaths don't generally feel well having to be "on" all day.

Of course, if you love what you do, whether it's sales or anything else, the situation might be different. One empath told me, "I can sell the merits of my professional pet-sitting business to anyone because I love it and believe in the benefits, but I can't sell a glass of water to a guy dying of thirst in the desert." Passion for your work can motivate you to overcome obstacles.

Other stressful careers for empaths include public relations, politics, executives who manage large teams, and being a trial attorney. These high-intensity professions value extroversion, the ability to engage in small talk, and an assertiveness or aggressiveness rather than being soft-spoken, sensitive, and introspective. They typically require responding to hundreds of daily emails and many phone calls, which can be overwhelming and anxiety-provoking for empaths. Preschool teachers and childcare workers must cope with the chaos and noise of crying babies and toddlers, which can also be draining—not to mention being a middle school vice principal.

The mainstream corporate world is problematic too. The "this is how it's done" corporate mentality is difficult for empaths, including myself. That response has always frustrated me because there's nowhere to go with it, and it clearly doesn't value an individual's needs. Empaths are independent thinkers who question the status quo when something doesn't feel right at work. They like to know the reasoning behind a decision so that they can make sense of it in their gut. Plus, regular team meetings and power-hungry teammates are draining for empaths.

Many empaths prefer not to travel for their jobs because of hectic airports, crowds, and strange hotels. But if travel is part of an empath's work, they need to practice self-care. One patient who runs online courses and attends many work-related conferences has dinner alone in her room to refuel herself. Another empath who often drives to different cities for her aromatherapy business told me, "My alone time comes on the road and in my hotel at night. I always pack candles for the room. During a longer stay, I buy flowers to make my room homey." A friend who is a flight attendant told me, "I adore travel, but I have to stagger my trips rather than planning them back to back. I also carry prayer symbols and talismans as protection from negative energy on flights." If you need to fly for work, you might want to get a pair of noise-canceling earbuds. One patient says, "I use them to block out the crying children, who are inevitably seated next to me." (You will find additional tips for travel in chapter 2.)

Even if your job is not ideal and you can't leave it, you can improvise and find solutions that make your situation more comfortable. One empath told me, "As a bus driver, I'm bombarded by energy from the public. So I play music on the bus and sing along with it. Music makes me happy and shields me from the stress I pick up from passengers. I also send them silent blessings to increase the positive energy. Before my shift, I walk up and down the bus with prayer bells to clear any negativity left over from previous trips." Just as this woman did, you can use the protection strategies in this book to clear negativity and create a greater sense of positivity in your workplace.

Working in Health Care and Other Helping Professions

Empaths are naturals for the helping professions, from medicine to teaching. These jobs feed our giving nature and provide opportunities to tap our sensitivities to offer others healing and insight. As a psychiatrist, it has been enormously fulfilling for me to work with patients, many of whom are empaths, and watch their anxieties lift so that they can love their lives without guarding their hearts. Numerous empaths in the helping professions share the gratification I experience and greatly benefit from devoting their careers to service.

Unfortunately, many also burn out. Empaths and other healers can experience compassion fatigue, a stress-related condition in which they've cared so much for so many people that there's nothing left to give. How does this happen? They overgive. They take on people's pain. They try to fix others and feel too responsible for the progress of their patients or whomever they're guiding. They also take it personally when someone doesn't progress, gets worse, or gives up. For instance, I've known substance-abuse counselors who feel responsible when a client relapses. Other mistakes that well-meaning healers also make are to schedule appointments every hour, year after year, without centering themselves by meditating or resting between sessions. Also, they overbook their free time and don't play enough or recharge themselves outside work. When empathic people neglect self-care, it's hard for them to survive in the helping professions, let alone feel the joy of giving.

One college student at my intuition workshop asked me, "Are empaths too sensitive to be in the healing arts? My desire to be of service conflicts with my desire to protect my energy." "The sensitivity of empaths can make them talented healers," I explained. "But to avoid burnout, we need daily strategies to recharge ourselves and safeguard our energy. Then we won't be drained by patients or coworkers."

Here are some self-care suggestions to practice both at and away from work. They will protect you from compassion fatigue because you aren't constantly absorbing people's stress, emotions, or physical symptoms.

Tips to Prevent Burnout and Compassion Fatigue

1. **Plan breaks.** Take regular five-minute breaks to rest, meditate, or enjoy a walk between appointments. Be careful not to schedule clients back to back, which will quickly lead to burnout.

2. **Don't overbook yourself.** If possible, limit the number of clients you see to what feels right, though some jobs may not allow that flexibility. When you're busy, try not to squeeze in new appointments if you can reschedule them for a lighter day.

3. **Eat well.** Don't skip meals, and make sure they include protein, which grounds you. Grazing on protein throughout the day keeps my energy and blood sugar stable. Avoid carbohydrates, candy bars, cookies, sodas, and other sugar sources, as well as fast food for a quick fix when you're hungry. Instead, bring healthy snacks and stay well hydrated with water, a green or antioxidant smoothie, and other nourishing drinks. (See chapter 3 for more food suggestions.)

4. **Create a serene workspace.** Have a peaceful office or at least a peaceful desk if you're in an open-space arrangement. Surround yourself with inspirational sayings and sacred objects and anything else that brings you peace.

5. **Practice deep breathing regularly.** Mindful deep breathing clears the negativity you pick up.

6. **Fill your office or workspace with heart energy.** Once or more daily, take a few minutes to focus on your heart chakra, which is in the middle of your chest. Feel that loving energy flow through your body as it balances you. Know that in doing this, the loving energy will overflow and fill the room, as though fairy dust has been sprinkled everywhere. It imbues a location with warmth and positivity. I've used this technique for years to create a loving atmosphere in my office. When visitors enter your space, they will relax and even smile without knowing why.

7. **Set clear boundaries at work.** Firmly and kindly say "no" to the energy vampires in your workplace. Protect your time so you are not drained.

8. **Shield yourself.** In stressful situations or if you are picking up someone else's emotions or symptoms, picture a shield of white light all around you that protects you and allows in only what is positive. This strategy works well for all healthcare professionals,

including massage therapists, physical therapists, and other bodyworkers, who are vulnerable to absorbing their patients' pain though physical touch. One dentist told me he uses the shield to protect himself from absorbing his patient's anxiety about a procedure. Shielding doesn't reduce your sensitivities or your ability to connect with those you're helping. It simply prevents their stress and anxiety from affecting you.

9. **Detoxify in water.** Take Epsom salt baths or shower after a long day to wash away the stress and pain you might have absorbed.

10. **Have fun outside work.** Allow regular time for play and "re-creation." Walking in nature while you enjoy flowers, plants, birdsong, and the rest of the natural world can revive your joy. Rather than thinking about patients or obsessing about job-related problems, be fully present during your play and recreation time.

The more you use these strategies, the more energized you'll feel and the less prone you'll be to burnout. Then you can really feel the passion and thrill of helping others. One empath, who usually loves running an assisted-care facility for seniors, was on the verge of burnout until she started to use the shielding visualization. Once she stopped absorbing the ever-present stress in that setting, the joy in her work returned. Along with the above strategies, you might want to check out my audio program *Becoming an Intuitive Healer*, which I designed for helping professionals. It offers self-care guidance as well.

The Empathic Therapist

Empathic psychotherapists, including psychiatrists, psychologists, marriage and family counselors, and social workers use intuition, empathy, and spirituality, along with their conventional training, to help others. They also teach their patients to become more intuitive and aware of energy. These therapists may be empaths, highly sensitive people, or practitioners who want to develop their empathic skills. The advantage of working with highly sensitive or empath therapists is that they can see more, feel more, and intuit more about patients, which enhances the psychotherapy process. We can connect with intuition and spirit, which helps us guide the people we are blessed to treat.

When I train healthcare professionals to incorporate empathy into their practices, they learn to tap in to the power of intuition—the still, small voice inside that offers clarity about health and healing. We contact it by becoming quiet within and then listening to any aha! moments of realization, flashes of knowing, gut feelings, and body sensations that are informing us. I view intuition as an expression of our highest self, or Spirit. Therapists who are empaths don't need to have traditional religious beliefs, though some do. However, it is necessary that they listen to their intuition and feel a higher power flowing through them—whether they understand that to be the universe, love, nature, or whatever instinctively resonates for them.

The healthcare professionals I train also learn how to read their patients' subtle energies, which is another therapeutic tool for diagnosis and treatment. This is a radically different perspective from the psychiatric training I received at UCLA, which was biologically oriented and medication based. Combining the knowledge of conventional science and the wisdom of intuitive medicine provides a great service.

As a therapist who is also an empath, I prepare for my sessions by meditating so that I can be calm and focused. Then I'm able to listen to what my patients are saying with my analytical mind and my intuition. I set aside my own problems and personal issues to be fully present with them. During a session, my patient is the center of my universe. This kind of selfless service energizes me. It also allows me to hear my intuition more deeply without extraneous thoughts interfering.

My role is to guide patients on the right course for their unique paths. It is not to fix them. When they suffer, I am right there shining light and offering direction. I realize that most emotional pain doesn't lift immediately, so I honor the different phases of healing. I don't rush my patients because I am uncomfortable with their pain. I don't need to take away their pain, and I don't indulge their wallowing in it. I also don't take responsibility for their growth. It is their job to change and grow. Mine is to inspire the process and help them listen to the wisdom of their intuition along the way. This attitude allows me to be a conduit for healing and protects me from absorbing someone's struggles and pain.

Here's an example of how I work. Jen, a forty-year-old interior designer, came to me with a history of painful relationships with narcissistic men. She would tolerate the abuse for far too long, then they would leave her, and it would take her months to recover. Jen wanted to change this destructive pattern.

In our first session, she told me about a man she had been dating for two weeks. "Craig is charming, funny, and a Harvard-educated attorney," she gushed. "He is my perfect man. He's different from my previous boyfriends because he listens to me." Everything about Craig delighted her. I wanted to be happy for Jen, but I also realized how hard it is to see the real person when you're infatuated with someone. (A friend jokes that at the start of a romance, the person is just sending a "representative.") As I tuned in to Craig, I received loud intuitive warnings that their relationship would be painful for her. I didn't share this with Jen though, because my intuition told me that doing so wouldn't have been useful. My job wasn't to predict her future but to assist her in making her own best decisions about relationships. So I responded, "Great! But get to know him better to make sure he's not like the other narcissists you've dated. Initially, you thought they were all fantastic too. What is your intuition saying about Craig?" Jen tried to tune in to her gut but could only feel her attraction for him, which she wrongly interpreted as a sign that they were meant to be.

My work with Jen was to help her connect with her intuition, despite her strong sexual attraction, which throws many of us off. Jen proceeded to enter a one-year relationship with Craig that was excruciating. After a few months, he became cold when she didn't do things his way. He gave her the silent treatment when he was angry. He threw her crumbs of love but then withdrew emotionally. These are all classic signs of a narcissist. This relationship was a hard yet vital lesson for Jen, about narcissists and their lack of empathy, despite the good show they put on during the honeymoon phase. Jen also learned the importance of using her intuition to evaluate possible partners and how she must keep trying to hear her inner voice until guidance comes, especially when she is thrown off-center.

In sessions, we focused on Jen reconnecting with her own power. As her sense of worth increased, she was finally able to say "no" to Craig, despite his attempts to reel her back with seductive promises of change. I was pleased when she gathered the strength to break the dysfunctional pattern and leave him.

She was determined to find a healthier relationship. The lessons Jen learned spurred her on to become a more insightful woman who valued her intuition. All relationships can be teachers and healers if we allow them to be.

I felt honored to serve as a light in Jen's time of darkness. It would not have been good for her or for me if I had absorbed her pain. Being clear about my therapeutic role protected me from taking on unwanted energies. During emotionally intense sessions, I breathed slowly and mindfully to stay centered. Both this strategy and setting clear boundaries allowed me to maintain optimal clarity in service to Jen.

Many of my empath patients who are also therapists feel just as passionate about their work as I do. One psychologist told me, "I love being in the zone, intuitively helping someone, trusting an inspiration I know is larger than myself." However, the biggest hazard of being an empathic therapist is the exhaustion that results if we don't safeguard against sensory overload and absorbing someone's emotions or physical ailments. One psychiatrist told me, "I pick up symptoms in my body from patients—headaches, nausea, back pain, depression, anger, and grief. It's overwhelming." Another patient shared, "As a mental health counselor, I couldn't turn off my empathy, so I left my job. Since then, I have felt happier and healthier, but something is missing in my life because psychotherapy is my calling."

Therapists who are empaths can also experience sensory overload from their work environment. A colleague who shares an office with me started to feel atypically anxious and tired. We discovered that he was sitting in the chair my patients sat in. He was picking up the stress that had accumulated there. He requested that I ask my patients to sit in the other chair. I totally understood his dilemma and agreed. After that, he felt calmer and more at ease in the office again.

How do empaths pursue their calling as healers and therapists without becoming sick, tired, or taking on their patient's symptoms? The following suggestions, along with others in this chapter, will help you stay centered and clear. All healthcare professionals can benefit from these strategies.

PROTECTION STRATEGY
How to Stop Taking on a Patient's Emotions

- **Adjust your attitude.** Don't become a martyr. Your role is to be a guide for your patients, not to take on their pain or remove it. When you're clear about this, you'll enjoy your work more and excel at it.

- **Identify three obvious differences between you and your patient.** A good intellectual way to distance yourself from a patient's emotions and pain after a session is to focus on three clear differences between you. For example, I'm a woman, and he's a man. She's depressed, but I'm not. I'm a vegan, and he eats meat. This lets you appreciate what's you and what's the patient, a boundary that helps prevent you from absorbing unwanted energy.

- **Don't try to fix others.** People heal themselves. You can support your patients' healing, but they must make the necessary changes to free themselves from suffering.

- **Watch out for codependency.** Be careful not to get hooked into feeling responsible for someone's progress. People change on their timeline, not yours. Of course, your heart will go out to patients who are emotionally stuck or backsliding. Guide them as much as possible, but you are not responsible for their growth or their ability to overcome obstacles.

- **Work on your own issues.** We tend to absorb energy that is related to issues we haven't resolved in ourselves. Compassionately notice when your patients push your own emotional buttons. Ask yourself, "Is this person mirroring issues in me that need healing?" Identify your triggers. Depression? Fear of abandonment? Fear of rejection? Anxiety about health? Intimacy? Focus on healing those triggers and issues in yourself. Then you won't be as apt to absorb these from others. Peer-oriented supervision groups where you can present cases and discuss what emotionally triggers you are helpful, as is working with your own therapist. ∎

Always stay centered in your heart with patients. Keep breathing out any discomfort you pick up, and return to your heart. The heart is the ultimate healer and purifier of all things. If you are emotionally triggered during a session, use shielding and other protective techniques to stay centered. Later you can investigate what triggered you and gain more insight about it. I love that as empaths and healers we need to stay current with our own growth. This necessity gives the psychotherapy process an integrity that benefits you and your patients. Be compassionate with yourself as you explore your own psyche and develop your empathic abilities. Enjoy this path of awakening in the spirit of love, service, and your own evolution.

—

I hope I have inspired you in the area of work. You can reinvigorate your current job or find work that is a better match for your needs as an empath. You have nothing to prove in your choice of career. It doesn't matter what kind of work you do as long as it satisfies you. Simply find a job that makes you happy. On stressful days, focus on your service to coworkers and others you come into contact with. This will allow negative energy to shift, putting you more at ease. Remember to view difficult people as teachers, which will help you stay grounded and not be as easily triggered. Stay aware of your needs and seek work that is in harmony with them. Practice ongoing self-care to cope with job stresses, to restore your energy, and just to pamper yourself. This will allow your empath heart to grow and be more fulfilled each day.

EMPATH AFFIRMATION

I set my intention to attract rewarding work that energizes me. I will practice self-care in my profession to protect my sensitivities. I vow to play and to rest when I'm off work to recharge myself.

Chapter 8

EMPATHS, INTUITION, AND EXTRAORDINARY PERCEPTIONS

Empaths perceive the world in such rich and multilayered ways. The great news is that our ability to witness the miraculous nature of life just keeps on deepening. As our sensitivities continue to awaken—and the safer we feel with them—the more we learn to expand our intuition to experience a range of wondrous perceptions.

Most people are intuitively tuned in to a narrow bandwidth of frequencies in the everyday material or "real world." Their ability to "see" is limited to linear time. But don't mistake the material plane for the only reality. Once your sensitivities can reach beyond it, you will enter a playground of subtler energies and fascinating "nonlocal" realms (a term used by consciousness researchers), which defy the laws of classical physics.

People I call intuitive empaths are especially able to receive nonlocal information. These super senses enrich their lives and connect them to the divine, putting them in touch with the magical timing of moments of synchronicity as well as experiences such as déjà vu, spirit guides, and angels. Some believe that these empaths are old souls, those who have seen much over the eons and have come into this life with highly developed intuition. Intuitive empaths differ from highly sensitive people in the area of intuition. Though both have a heightened awareness of touch, smell, sound, and light, intuitive empaths can sense further than local reality to contact extraordinary knowledge. They know things that other people don't because their channels are wide open. Some have visions that predict the future, and some are able to communicate with animals, plants, and other elements of nature, even spirit guides. Some are powerful dreamers who receive guidance in their dreams. Intuitive empaths can access the mysterious, nonlocal aspects of human consciousness, which mainstream science doesn't yet understand.

As an empath, you must learn to use the gifts of intuition wisely and remain grounded. Sometimes these experiences can feel far-out and overwhelming. The strategies in this chapter will help you stay centered and integrate what you see and feel in a healthy way.

In my psychiatric practice, I've experienced the fears and rewards of being an intuitive empath. These abilities serve me because I have greater insight into my patients, allowing me to quickly "read" them and other aspects of my

AS A CHILD I FELT MYSELF TO BE ALONE, AND I AM STILL, BECAUSE I KNOW THINGS AND MUST HINT AT THINGS THAT OTHERS APPARENTLY KNOW NOTHING OF, AND FOR THE MOST PART DO NOT WANT TO KNOW. LONELINESS DOES NOT COME FROM HAVING NO PEOPLE ABOUT ONE, BUT FROM BEING UNABLE TO COMMUNICATE THE THINGS THAT SEEM IMPORTANT TO ONESELF, OR FROM HOLDING CERTAIN VIEWS WHICH OTHERS FIND INADMISSIBLE.

Dr. Carl Jung

environment. I am also a passionate dreamer and follow the direction of my dreams to guide my life. In addition, I am deeply nurtured communing with nature and the elements—air, fire, water, and earth. I appreciate their beauty, but I can also feel each element's aliveness in my body, which is exhilarating.

During childhood, I was frightened by my intuitive empathy. At the time, I didn't even know there was a name for what I was experiencing. Along with being able to sense energy around people, I could predict illnesses, earthquakes, and other disasters, which was disconcerting. When I was nine, I predicted my dear grandfather's unexpected death. The night before he passed away, I had a dream in which he came to say good-bye, telling me, "I love you very much. Don't worry about me. I'm fine." When I woke, it was three in the morning, and I rushed into my parents' room to share the dream. My mother smiled and reassured me, "Sweetheart, it's only a nightmare," and then tucked me back into bed. But at breakfast, the telephone rang, and we got the sad news: Grandpop had died suddenly of a heart attack.

My parents wrote off my dream as a "weird coincidence." But I felt I had somehow caused or contributed to his death and that something was wrong with me. My conclusions were incorrect, but no one could tell me otherwise. So I was alone for many years, trying to understand this experience and my other intuitions, which created much anxiety, shame, and confusion. I felt lonely and isolated with no one to reassure me that I was okay. I have since found solace in Carl Jung's description of his childhood.

Given my background, I hope you can understand why it brings me such joy to put these experiences in a healthy context for you. You are not causing the events you are able to predict, and there is nothing wrong with you. Your sensitivities simply allow you to know certain things that defy logic and the limited definitions many people have of what is possible. Know that being an intuitive empath is natural, beautiful, full of wonder, and will connect you with all of life.

TYPES OF INTUITIVE EMPATHS

I've observed with my patients and workshop participants that intuitive empaths can manifest in different forms, which I will describe. See if you identify with one or more of these types. Sometimes you can begin as one type, and with practice, go on to develop the traits of other types too. As you learn about these abilities, try to release any programmed notions that they are impossible. Whether you believe intuition comes from your subconscious, your highest self, angels, spirit guides, or other helpers, stay open and playful while exploring your heightened sensitivities. Intuition facilitates the sacred art of connection, with yourself, others, and the universe.

Telepathic Empaths

Telepathic empaths can intuitively read what is happening with others in present time, even if a person's thoughts and feelings are unexpressed. They receive images, impressions, flashes, and knowings about loved ones, coworkers, clients, even strangers.

Here's what this phenomenon can look like. You're thinking about a close friend. Then the phone rings, and that friend is the caller. You sense that your daughter is sick, even though she lives a thousand miles away—and later learn that she is indeed sick. Or a wave of positive feeling washes over you, and then you discover that you've received that great new job offer you hoped for.

How can you tell if an intuition is accurate and not a projection of your own emotions and issues? Note whether the information you picked up has a neutral or compassionate tone. Be suspect of intuitive flashes with a high emotional charge or that reflect issues you are struggling with. To stay clear, you must know yourself well. For example, if a fear of abandonment is an emotional trigger for you and you keep sensing that a friend or maybe your partner is going to desert you, you are probably projecting your fear onto them. But if you get a matter-of-fact flash with a neutral tone that your coworker is going to leave her job, that insight is most likely accurate. You may be upset afterward because you don't want to lose this person, but the information didn't initially carry an emotional charge.

Being a telepathic empath can be overwhelming. One workshop participant who did hundreds of readings a week on a psychic hotline told me, "The sheer masses of people I read are exhausting. I use grounding techniques, but I'm still burned out. It's too much information to clear." Although she was in an unusually intense situation, you can also experience telepathy overload in your daily life. Intuitions come from many directions: you sense things about strangers in the grocery store, passersby on the street, coworkers, friends, as well as family members. You may not be tuning in intentionally, yet the intuitions still come. To avoid intuitive overload, stay grounded, shield yourself, and use the strategies I share in this chapter.

As a telepathic empath, the information you pick up allows you to develop both more insight and compassion for people. You can also help them if there's an opening to do so. It's a gift to feel this heightened connection to others' thoughts and feelings. Respect this gift always.

Precognitive Empaths

Precognitive empaths have premonitions about the future, either while they're awake or in their dreams. They may receive these premonitions spontaneously or when they intentionally tune in—a skill that can be developed with practice. You may receive premonitions about someone's health, relationships, career, or other issues. For instance, you might know if a friend will become ill, pass away, get married, or be accepted into college long before others do. Precognitive empaths are receiving this information from nonlocal realms; it doesn't originate in the linear world.

Some mystics call this nonlocal storehouse of collective information the Akashic Records, or Book of Life, which is said to contain all of human history—past, present, and future. Precognitive empaths can reach beyond linear reality to access this knowledge. There is mention of such records in the myths of many cultures as well as in the Old and New Testaments. Belief in these spiritual tablets can be traced back to ancient Assyria, Babylonia, India, Phoenicia, and to the Hebrews as well.

Precognitive empaths must be clear about how to use their foreknowledge with integrity. Sometimes you can warn others of a stressful or dangerous situation so that they will be more cautious or avoid it. With happier events, such as a couple becoming pregnant, you can say in a light tone, "My intuition tells me you will have a child soon." Know that the information about the future you're sensing is just a probability; there's always a chance you could be wrong because most futures aren't fixed. So don't think of yourself as an all-knowing authority.

Also realize that often the events you pick up can't be changed. Sometimes it isn't appropriate to mention what you intuit to someone. How do you make this decision? The answer is always about what will serve the person. Check in with your intuition and ask, "Is this information appropriate to share? Would it help this person to know?" Then listen for an intuitive yes or no, and follow that guidance. If you are unsure, keep your insights to yourself until a stronger message comes. I share about half the intuitions I receive about my patients with them. Some I never disclose because I sense it wouldn't benefit them. And with others, I wait until the time feels right for them to hear it. Well-meaning intuitives can scare people if they aren't mindful of their presentation or are motivated by ego and a desire to impress people with their talents. Always keep the other person's welfare foremost in your mind. To maintain the integrity of this gift, you must practice constraint and humility.

Precognitive empaths have many misconceptions about their gift. You may feel you are causing the events you predict or believe it is your responsibility to prevent them, especially deaths. Neither is true. Highly charged negative events and emotions simply emit louder signals. They are easier to sense than happier circumstances for untrained precognitive empaths. As you hone your intuition, you will be able to attune to a wider range of signals.

> SOME EMPATHS HAVE VERY STRONG INTUITION AND VISIONS THAT GUIDE THEIR LIVES.
> **Judith Orloff, MD**

Dream Empaths

Dream empaths regularly have vivid dreams that they remember, an experience that frequently starts in childhood. If you're a dream empath you are attracted to the dreamworld and look forward to sleeping each night. Dreams are such a powerful form of intuition because they bypass the ego and the linear mind to offer clear intuitive information. They bring guidance about healing, spirituality, and overcoming difficult emotions (sometimes through the healing power of nightmares), telling you how to help yourself and others.

In addition, your dreams can be telepathic or precognitive, relaying information about both current issues and future ones. One patient told me, "I have dreamed about what will be in the headlines the next day, from an actress winning an award to a drive-by shooting." Also, you may get flashes of someone else's dreams when you're talking to the person. Because these empaths are so in sync with dreams, they have more access to this realm than other people.

Like some dream empaths, you may have spirit guides, who communicate with you during sleep. They appear in many forms, such as animals, people, presences, angels, or loving voices. They can tell you how to overcome obstacles, reach your goals, or lead a more spiritual and peaceful life. Not everyone has specific spirit guides; if you do, be sure to listen to them. They provide helpful, compassionate information—never anything that is harmful to others or to you.

Dream empaths can travel to other realms in dreamtime. I've been a dream empath since childhood. I feel more comfortable in dreams than I do awake. Each day I can only operate in the material world for so long. Then I need to be with the sacredness of the dreamworld, which nourishes me.

As a dream empath, you can develop your abilities. Keep a dream journal and write down your dreams every morning. Upon awakening, spend a few quiet moments in the hypnagogic state, the state between sleeping and waking, and record whatever snatches of your dreams that you remember. Then you can meditate on the meaning of this information throughout the day. My book *Emotional Freedom* describes in detail how to remember and interpret dreams. Also, get in the habit of asking a question before you go to sleep, anything from "What direction shall I take in my career?" to "Is this relationship good for me?" In the morning, see how the answer in the dream applies to your question. Regularly remembering and learning from your dreams will help you more deeply understand yourself and others. You may also want to practice lucid dreaming, a technique that shamans use. In this state, you are aware of being in your dream while you are having it. You are able to observe what is going on in the dream and to direct the outcome.

Using all these methods, I consider dreamwork a devotional act for sensitive people, which honors our intuition, spirituality, and the reality of other dimensions.

Mediumship Empaths

These empaths can communicate with people, animals, and spirits on the Other Side. They have a special talent for reaching over the great divide and bridging the gap between this life and the hereafter.

Mediumship is a resonance with what lies beyond the material plane. The ordinary boundaries that separate "here" from "there" aren't a deterrent. These types of empaths are channels who can set aside their intellectual minds and egos to allow intuitive messages to come through them. They function in the same way a telephone wire does. If you identify with this type of empathy, mediumship is a skill you can develop with practice and the proper guidance from a skilled teacher.

Whether you are communicating with someone's deceased Uncle Fred or someone's sweet departed poodle, the messages are often similar. Those on the Other Side want us to know that they are fine, that their spirits have more work to do there, and that they love us. I had a session with a medium in England who told me, "You have more friends in the afterlife than you do in this life," which rang true and made me laugh. Certain mediums are channels for angels, such as Archangel Michael, who is a protector and instills faith in spirit. I've seen how consulting a medium can be therapeutic for people who are grieving. Though this ability is not understood or accepted by modern science, mediums have existed throughout history and around the world. Some are shams, but others feel authentic.

If you are this kind of empath, you can communicate with the Other Side by first opening your heart in a meditative state. Love traverses all boundaries, so when you set that tone, you can be heard across universes. Next, identify the person you want to reach and inwardly ask to contact them. Then be open to auditory, visual, or other kinds of messages you receive. The process is like communicating with anyone else except that this person is pure energy. I sometimes meditate on my parents who have passed on, to connect with them more deeply, an experience that consoles me and brings us closer. Sometimes they have guidance for me.

However, like other intuitive experiences, this one can feel overwhelming too. Communicating with the Other Side can happen spontaneously to sensitive children and untrained adults, which may feel scary or out of control. Think of Whoopi Goldberg's hilarious character Oda Mae Brown in the classic film *Ghost*. She was a medium who had crowds of spirits jumping into her to deliver messages to loved ones, and they overwhelmed her!

To stay calm and centered, it's essential to practice the grounding and shielding techniques I've discussed. In addition, realize that you have the right to say "no" to any experience you don't want. You may need to set boundaries with those on the Other Side just as you do with people on this side. Once you begin to see mediumship as a natural extension of your empathy and intuition, you'll feel more comfortable setting limits and practicing the self-care techniques that are necessary to maintain all healthy relationships.

Plant Empaths

Plant empaths have a natural attraction to plants, trees, and flowers. They intuitively connect with their needs and communicate with their spirits. They can sense if plants are healthy and what is required to heal them when they're not.

If you're this kind of empath, plants talk to you, and you can hear them. You are drawn to the woods, mountains, and bodies of water to be close to nature. When you were a child, trees and plants were your companions and confidants. You might have turned to them with your problems or for solace when you were upset, as I did while growing up. Just being close to a tree is reassuring for plant empaths. You like to touch them, climb them, hug them, and sometimes just say hello when you're walking by.

Plant empaths often have a green thumb; plants and flowers flourish around you. They feel your ability to attune to them. This mutual kinship makes them responsive to your touch and presence. That's why many plant empaths enjoy gardening or enter careers in farming, horticulture, botany, garden design, landscape architecture, floral arranging, or working for the Forest Service. To feel healthy and happy, these empaths need to be near plants and the natural world.

Plant empaths also become healers, such as Chinese medical practitioners or herbalists. Some prescribe flower remedies, a form of homeopathy developed by Dr. Edward Bach in which flower essences are distilled in liquid form to treat various kinds of diseases. In ancient times, when people lived in harmony with nature, they regarded plants as sentient, aware, and intelligent. Then and now, tribal shamans and curanderos act as messengers between plants and the spirit world. They hear the beautiful songs of plants and can tap in to the healing powers of plant medicine.

If you identify with this type of empath, you are able to receive guidance from plants and feel their divinity. You can look deeply into a flower or a tree and receive information, a technique that shamans call "gazing." You can meditate beside a plant, ask it any question, and then intuitively receive an answer. Plants convey everything from personal and spiritual guidance to messages that help others and the world. They are compassionate and giving beings.

The challenge of being a plant empath is that you may feel the pain of green living things. You know when they are hurting or dying. You feel the anguish of forests that have been destroyed by humanity. Your own body hurts when plants are harmed. To release this pain, you must acknowledge these emotions and physical sensations, breathe the discomfort out of your body, and keep sending love and blessings to the plant world across the globe.

Earth Empaths

Earth empaths are attuned to the earth and the changes in their bodies. Sensually and energetically, they can feel the power of a thunderstorm, the loveliness of the moon, and the warmth of the sun. If you are this type of empath, what happens to the earth is intimately connected to your body. The beauty and health of the earth nourishes and sustains you. The ocean and tides affect everyone, but especially you. You are sensitive to changes in the weather and daylight. Earth empaths may be more prone to Seasonal Affective Disorder, becoming depressed in the winter when the days are shorter and darker.

The earth, its elements, and the universe feel like family to you. The moon and stars have always been my companions. A woman in my workshop once told me that she prefers stargazing to bars and clubs as her form of nightlife. Since childhood, I've looked up at the heavens and felt that my true home was there. I've found that empaths who, like me, have a hard time adjusting to being on this planet need to connect to the earth's energy so that we can more fully inhabit our bodies. Learning how to do this is part of our healing.

If you are this kind of empath, your body is intimately connected to the earth. You can feel how much the earth loves us. You experience her changes as if they were happening to you. That's why you may feel hurt, anxious, or experience health problems if she is harmed. When the earth is happy, you're happy, and when she is in pain, you are too.

Earth empaths often have premonitions about natural disasters or feel them intensely in their bodies as they are occurring. One patient told me, "I frequently wake up just before an earthquake. Then boom! It hits." Another said, "Before an earthquake or volcanic eruption, my body begins to shake. I feel off, like I'm not on solid ground." Yet another told me, "During the last tsunami, I woke from a deep sleep in a state of agitation and dread." And one empath friend said she felt like she was hemorrhaging after a catastrophic oil spill. Be aware of how your body reacts to dramatic earth changes. Then you can put your feelings in context and practice more self-care when they occur.

Earth empaths may also be sensitive to solar flares. These magnetic storms on the sun affect the magnetic fields around the earth as well as around our bodies. Earthquakes, volcanic eruptions, hurricanes, and tornados appear to occur after intense solar activity. During these periods, you may experience headaches, mood swings, anxiety, or heart palpitations. Studies have shown an association between solar flares and increased depression, anxiety, suicides, and episodes of bipolar disorder.[1] Revolutions, riots, and unrest across the globe are also associated with solar flares. Remember, the sun is responsible for life on earth, so when it goes through changes, we feel it ninety-three million miles away. This experience is amplified for empaths.

To stay vibrant and maximize these abilities, you need to frequently connect with the earth. Spend time in forests, by the ocean, or in the mountains, where you can commune with the elements and feel at home. To deepen your bond with the earth, also eat clean, healthy, organic foods—better yet, grow them yourself. A diet of junk food separates us from the earth because we're not ingesting her energy. Also remember to regularly practice Earthing, especially lying flat on the earth to soak up her strength and positivity. Walk barefoot on the grass. Wade or swim in lakes, rivers, or the ocean. Gaze at the stars.

To intentionally communicate with the earth, tune in to her and ask, "What do you feel?" Then be open to any intuitions that come. You can also use the earth as an oracle and ask her questions about yourself or others. She will answer you through your intuition, and when she does, follow her guidance.

In native traditions, Mother Earth is revered and cared for, and earth medicine is the healing that nature imparts. You can practice earth medicine by doing whatever you can to treasure our precious planet. This is part of our purpose, and an important way for an earth empath to feel happy, healthy, and whole.

Animal Empaths

Animal empaths have a special ability to tune in to animals and communicate with them. They may even have a specific gift, such as being a "horse whisperer" or "dog whisperer." If you identify with this type, you can sense when animals feel worried, upset, lonely, or unsafe. By understanding their emotions, you can offer them healing support. You seem to attract animals wherever you go and adore being in their presence. So you may work in rescue shelters, advocate for animal rights, practice veterinary medicine, or help animals in other ways.

Animal empaths, who are also known as animal communicators, have been present throughout history. Saint Francis of Assisi, the patron saint of animals, was able to talk to "his sisters and brothers," including rabbits, deer, and fish, and he was famous for taming a wolf. Creatures of all kinds flocked to him, as is portrayed in sacred art. He often went into periods of seclusion with only animal companions, which is typical for introverted empaths. He was known for giving sermons to audiences of birds. St. Francis said of the animals, "We have a higher mission—to be of service to them whenever they require it."

As an animal empath, you realize that animals are highly empathic with us, that they feel our emotions and intentions too. For instance, your dog or cat knows when you are sad or in pain and responds with unconditional love. Also, because you are so attuned to animals, you can receive intuitive guidance from them, such as warnings about your safety or omens of happiness. Indigenous peoples believe that animals hear our thoughts. You may be able to hear theirs as well. You know what they need and can respond to them. Animal empaths are devoted champions of their well-being.

The Power of Animal Medicine

Intuitive empaths—and indeed all types of sensitive people—can benefit from the wisdom and protection of animals. In Native American culture, animal medicine imparts the healing lessons that specific animals bring us. Once you become aware of such a lesson, you can make appropriate changes in your life. For instance, dolphins represent peace, harmony, and play. So if you spot a pod of dolphins, it's a sign to bring those traits out in yourself. Spider medicine represents creativity, and ant medicine is about patience and perseverance. Pay attention to the creatures that keep showing up on your path. Listen for their teaching.

Shamans say that animals can be our allies in stressful or dangerous situations. This is a valuable resource for empaths. I recommend the following meditation to call on the power of the jaguar to protect you. I use it when I need extra protection, especially if too much negativity is coming at me too fast. The jaguar is a fierce and patient guardian that can keep draining people and energy away.

PROTECTION STRATEGY
The Jaguar Meditation

Find a quiet environment where you can't be interrupted. Sit in a comfortable position. Take a few deep breaths to center yourself and let go of stress. In this calm state, from deep within your heart, call on the spirit of the jaguar to protect you. Feel its presence enter. Then visualize this gorgeous, powerful creature patrolling your energy field, encircling it, protecting you, and keeping intruders and any negative forces out. Picture what the jaguar looks like—its beautiful, fierce, and loving eyes; its sleek body; the graceful and purposeful way it moves. Feel secure in the circle of its protection.

As you close this meditation, give inner thanks to the jaguar. Know that you can call on it whenever there is a need. Feel the power of that. Then slowly and gently open your eyes. Orient yourself back to current time and space. Completely return to your own body, and be alert, aware, and present in your environment.

In addition to this meditation with the jaguar, you might also want to experiment reaching out to other animals you resonate with in similar meditations. ■

As an intuitive empath, the more you open, the more you can receive visions and guidance from nonlinear realms. This information will enrich your life and the lives of those you assist. Some intuitive empaths also experience visitations from angels and benefit from their divine intervention. If you can relate to this, get into the habit of calling on the angels for guidance and protection. This connection will help to make the process of contacting different realms feel safer and more fun.

PROTECTING YOURSELF
FROM INTUITIVE OVERLOAD

Just as empaths can experience sensory overload in daily life, intuitive empaths can experience overload from nonlocal input. Basically, our empathy goes into high gear, and we can't shut it off. How does this manifest? We're bombarded by intuitive information everywhere we go and then become exhausted by the onslaught of energies we sense. When we have frighteningly accurate dreams and premonitions, with outcomes we can't change, we experience the stress of that. To avoid getting overwhelmed, we need to pace ourselves. I offer the following suggestions to help you stay grounded.

PROTECTION STRATEGY
Tips to Protect Yourself from Intuitive Overload

- **Dialogue with your inner voice.** You can always ask your inner voice to slow down so that you can take a break or find a rhythm that's more comfortable. Intuition doesn't just happen to us. You can cultivate an active and conscious connection with it.

- **Develop a witness state.** When you tune in, try to stay neutral. In many situations, the role of an empath is simply to bear witness—a sacred duty that the ancient prophets understood. You might wonder: Why am I sensing death, illness, or other painful circumstances at all? What good is it if I can't prevent them? Keep in mind that the act of *seeing* in itself bears light. Sometimes it's not your job to intervene, nor is it possible. In those situations, you can always hold the light for people and send them blessings. This is a holy act that supports others in miraculous ways.

- **You are not responsible for the karma of others.** Keep reminding yourself that everyone deserves the dignity of walking their own path. This will help you avoid feeling inappropriately responsible for what you intuitively sense.

- **Visualize light.** Picture divine white light coming though the crown of your head, as darkness flows out the bottom of your feet. This process reduces overwhelm by circulating positive energy into your body and releasing toxic energy. ▪

As you gain confidence in your intuition, you'll be less likely to feel overwhelmed by your experiences. Along with the above tips, I suggest also using the strategies I shared in chapter 5 that address any codependency issues you might have on an intuitive level. All of these will keep you focused, clear, and empowered. The wonder of being an intuitive empath is that you're open to exploring realms beyond the linear. As your particular sensitivities grow, the more deeply you can explore the many levels of consciousness.

Whenever we contact intuition, we are in sacred time, not linear reality. The ancient Greeks had two concepts of time. *Chronos* is clock-time, which is measured in seconds, minutes, hours, months, and years. Throughout history, it has largely been represented by Father Time, a tired, stooped, and bearded old man carrying a scythe and an hourglass. He resembles the grim reaper. Chronos is often regarded as a realm wrought with conflict and difficulties.

On the other hand, *Kairos* is sacred time, which refers to the right or supreme moment when opportune events can occur. It is a nonsequential and infinite state, outside of linear time and space. You may know it as "being in the zone." Kairos is the realm where synchronicities happen, those moments of perfect timing. It is also the realm of déjà vu, that sense of familiarity with a place or person you've not encountered before in linear time. Kairos is the magical location of timeless, mystical wisdom. You can't travel to it using a physical map, but it can be reached with intuition. Kairos is the domain of intuitive empaths. As you develop your abilities, you'll find that a range of intuitive experiences will feel more natural and comfortable to you.

EMPATH AFFIRMATION

I will honor my intuition.
I will listen to my dreams.
I will not second-guess my inner voice.
I will seek to find balance with my
intuition and other aspects of
my life so that I can express
my full spectrum of
sensitivities and
be whole.

Chapter 9

THE GIFT OF BEING AN EMPATH

The empath's journey is the adventure of a lifetime. Sensitive people have much to be grateful for. You are able to experience exquisite passion and joy. You can perceive the big picture on a deep level. You are attuned to the beauty, poetry, and energy of life, and your compassion gives you the capacity to help others. You are not callous, shut off, or cold-hearted. Your sensitivities allow you to be a caring, vulnerable, and aware being.

Empaths have a special relationship to nature. You feel a kinship with animals, flowers, trees, and clouds. You are drawn to the peace of the wilderness, the quiet of the desert, the majesty of the red rock canyons and the forests, and the vastness of the ocean. You can dance under the full moon and feel her loveliness in your body. You know how to be at one with the serenity of nature. You want to protect the earth, our mother, and conserve her precious resources.

As empaths, you also have the power to positively change yourself, your family, and the rest of the world. In my medical practice, I've seen how empaths are often "chosen" to break the generational patterns of negativity in their families. They don't necessarily volunteer for this role on a conscious level, but it's nonetheless their destiny to fulfill it. When empaths heal themselves and say "yes" to honoring their sensitivities, they are saying "no" to patterns of abuse, neglect, and addiction that have been repeated in their relatives. The intergenerational transmission of pain stops with them. Through their recovery and the acceptance of their gifts, empaths are the ones who can repair the greater familial whole. Mindful, conscious people are the most effective agents of change.

MOVE TOWARD THE LIGHT

The earth is not an enlightened planet. It is filled with tremendous suffering as well as tremendous joy. Our role as empaths is to use our sensitivities for the greater good and to tip the balance toward the light. Empaths must become warriors of light. Don't let the dark scare you. Trust the power of compassion. We need you to raise the vibration of the world. Children and adults change for the better when they are around others with strong, loving, and sensitive energy. You can embody that. The only obstacle that keeps you from shining is fear. As empaths, it is our assignment to gradually heal our fears so that they don't block our way to the light. As you do so, remember that you are not alone. You have angels and protection around you.

By being vulnerable and strong, empaths represent a new model of leadership. We can have a huge effect on humanity by promoting mutual understanding, the path to peace in our personal lives and globally. But such revolutions will last only when the revolutionaries lead by doing their own inner emotional and spiritual work. Then the positive political, social, and environmental changes we need are possible. Through our sensitivity we can create a compassion revolution and save the world.

I love when the environmentalist David Orr says, "The planet does not need more 'successful people.' The planet desperately needs more peacemakers, healers, restorers, storytellers, and lovers of all kinds. It needs people to live well in their places. It needs people with moral courage willing to join the struggle to make the world habitable and humane, and these qualities have little to do with success as our culture defines it."

Empaths are pivotal to manifesting this shift. Sensitivity is the path to nonviolence. We can be the healers and restorers and seers and lovers if we keep our sensitivities open and stay centered in our power. We don't have to be afraid of who we are. My advice to you is to do good and be good—the rest will follow. A commitment to this goal is critical because there is a quickening in the world now, a speeding up of time that mystics say will bring a reckoning of the light versus the dark on our planet. We need to take a loving stand. The more empowered you become, the more you can embody the change that the world needs.

CELEBRATING YOUR GIFTS

Throughout your life, continue to clarify the ways your empathy serves you, others, and the greater whole. The following exercise will help you remember these instances of empathy in action, and it is also a way of saying "thank you" for your gift.

SELF-REFLECTION EXERCISE

Embracing Your Empathy

It's helpful to be empathic many times throughout each day. Take a moment to reflect on the benefits this offers.

- Remember a time when you were able to empathize with your spouse's pain and you helped him or her with the depth of love you offered.

- Remember a time when you tuned in to your intuition and just *knew* what the best choice was. By listening to your inner voice, you were able to pick the right job, the right relationship, or the right teacher.

- Remember a time when you were afraid and didn't know what to do. But instead of putting yourself down or obsessing on the fear, you showed empathy and compassion for yourself. This loving attitude got you through the fearful period.

- Remember a time when a friend experienced a terrible relationship breakup and you loved and supported your friend though the pain.

- Remember how as a parent, an educator, or a caregiver, you were able to encourage a child to express their sensitivities and not to be ashamed of them. Be happy that you could enhance a child's life in this way.

THE POWER OF COMMUNITY

In addition to recognizing and embracing your gifts, I also recommend finding a community of like-minded people. Sensitive
souls are, by nature, what I call "co-empathic," which means
our sensitivities can be amplified in wonderful ways when we're
around other positive and sensitive people. In this regard, the
power of ten is greater than the power of one.

To reinforce each other's gifts and offer mutual understanding, I
encourage you to form an empath support group in your location.
It can consist of a few people or more. The beauty of community
is that we can help one another.
Being "seen" by even one person
brings great solace to a sensitive
soul. Coming together also offers
a healthy perspective on managing our sensitivity. Empaths tend
to take themselves quite seriously
because life feels so overwhelming, but this only increases their
stress. However, veteran empaths,
who have traveled this path and
learned coping strategies, can
show those awakening to their
sensitivities how to lighten up
and how to find amazing solutions to dilemmas that don't have
to overwhelm them. A support
group can provide merciful relief

> ALTHOUGH I AM
> A TYPICAL LONER
> IN MY DAILY LIFE,
> MY AWARENESS OF
> BELONGING TO THE
> INVISIBLE COMMUNITY
> OF THOSE WHO STRIVE
> FOR TRUTH, BEAUTY,
> AND JUSTICE HAS
> PREVENTED ME FROM
> FEELINGS OF ISOLATION.
> **Albert Einstein**

and grounding when we are on sensory overload. I say more about
getting a group started in the section "Creating Community: Setting
Up Your Own Empath Support Group" at the back of the book.

THE PATH TO INNER PEACE

In your own growth process, remember that the path to self-acceptance, inner peace, and spiritual growth is not a straight line. It's a spiral. We keep returning to issues we thought we had healed—but this time around, more profound truths are revealed, which enhance our self-knowledge. It's what makes this path so exciting for me. I yearn to move closer to the light. Delving more deeply into the spiral of my life and the consciousness of love takes me there. Empaths embrace depth. Though self-awareness often makes us stretch beyond our comfort zone—it's painful at times—the result is that we become more radiant, compassionate, and solid in our connection to spirit. There is no human attainment more precious than this. Every morning upon awakening, I inwardly ask to re-enter the kingdom of spirit and the heart. Then I know I'm in my right place in the universe to start the day.

Using the techniques in *The Empath's Survival Guide,* you can conquer the challenges of being sensitive and enjoy the journey. Reflect on the changes that you've experienced already since you've started reading this book. Notice how your life and relationships have improved when you embrace yourself as an empath. Celebrate your progress every time you listen to your intuition, assert your needs, or center yourself in the midst of chaos. Celebrate that you are no longer willing to deny your feelings just to make other people comfortable. Celebrate your ability to love your beautiful self today, without conflict or second-guessing. Be grateful for your progress. Baby steps are golden. Don't worry when you backslide. We all do sometimes. In every circumstance, treat yourself with compassion.

As an empath, you are part of a countercultural revolution to put what is *humane* back into *humanity*. I applaud you for being a path-forger, willing to venture off the beaten track. I applaud your courage to face yourself, to express your authentic needs, and not to give up on the world, with its many failings.

We are all part of the empath family, connected by our sensitivities and heart. So let's draw on each other's strength and loving-kindness. Let's feel comfort in the simple knowing that we each exist and that in our hearts we support one another from near and far. Even though many of us have not yet met, I send you all blessings and thanks for being brave enough to be authentically you.

In closing, I offer this final affirmation for you to honor your sensitivities again and again on this journey.

EMPATH AFFIRMATION

I will treasure myself and vow to have people in my life who treasure me as well. I will use my sensitivities to better my own life and the world. I will celebrate the adventure of being an empath.

PROTECTION STRATEGIES
A Quick Reference Guide

R efer to this summary of protection strategies whenever you need to easily access a range of options to protect yourself from exhaustion and overwhelm. The key to self-care is to recognize when you're experiencing the first signs of sensory overload or when you start absorbing negativity or stress from others. The sooner you can act to reduce stimulation and to center yourself, the more balanced and protected you will be.

Also, with all of the visualizations and meditations I present in this book, remember that it may be helpful to read the directions into a tape recorder with appropriate pauses. Then when you're ready to practice the meditation, you can simply play it back for yourself and relax into it.

1. Shielding Visualization

Shielding is a quick way to protect yourself. Many empaths rely on it to block out toxic energy, while allowing the flow of positive energy. Use it regularly. The minute you're uncomfortable with a person, a place, or a situation, put up your shield. Use it in a train station, at a party, when you're faced with an energy vampire, in a doctor's waiting room, or anywhere you feel uncomfortable.

Allow at least five minutes for this exercise. Find a quiet and protected space. Make sure that you won't be interrupted.

Loosen your clothing and find a position that's comfortable, perhaps sitting cross-legged on the floor or maybe upright on a chair. Begin by taking a few deep, long breaths. Breathe in, really feeling the inhalation, and then exhale, really letting out a big exhalation. Feel the sensuality of the breath, the connection to prana, the sacred life force.

Let all thoughts drift by like clouds in the sky, returning to your breath over and over again to find your center. Feel a core of energy running from your toes, throughout your body, and up through the top of your head. Focusing on this will keep you centered.

Now, as you're breathing, visualize a beautiful shield of white or pink light that surrounds your body completely and extends a few inches beyond it. This shield protects you from anything negative, stressful, toxic, or unwelcome. Within the protection of this shield, feel yourself centered, happy, and energized. This shield blocks out negativity, though at the same time it allows you to still feel what is positive and loving. Get used to the sensation of the shield protecting your body. You can visualize it at any moment when you suspect you're absorbing someone else's energy. Inwardly say "thank you" for this protection. To close, take a long, deep breath in and out, and then slowly open your eyes. Come back to the room. Be in your body completely.

2. Grounding and Earthing Visualization

When you feel overloaded, create some quiet time alone to lower your stimulation level. Being alone to recharge will help you decompress. Practice this visualization to return to your center. I use it for at least five minutes daily and teach it to my patients.

Close the door, and turn off the computer and phone. Then sit in a comfortable position and take a few deep breaths to relax your body. Start to feel still and at ease, as tension melts away. Nothing to do. Nothing to be. Just breathing and relaxing. When thoughts come, let them drift by like clouds in the sky. Do not attach to them. Focus only on slowly inhaling, and then exhaling. Feel stress leave your body as you connect to a sense of serenity.

In this tranquil inner place, visualize a large tree with a strong trunk extending down the center of your body, from head to toe. Take a few moments to feel its power and vibrant energy. Then visualize the tree's roots growing from the bottom of your feet, rooting down into the ground, making their way deeper and deeper to create a wonderful feeling of solidity. Let the roots anchor you into Mother Earth, stabilizing and centering you. Know that this "inner tree" will provide an inner strength to keep you safe and protected when life gets overwhelming.

3. Tips to Relieve Adrenal Fatigue

Overcoming adrenal fatigue requires some basic lifestyle and diet changes so that you can effectively manage your energy over the long term. Along with the following tips, refer to many other strategies I share throughout the book.

- **Eat a whole-food diet.** Avoid processed or junk food, sugar, gluten, and white flour. You can learn more in chapter 3.

- **Add Himalayan Red Salt to your diet.** Eliminate low-quality salts. Always check with your physician if your blood pressure is high.

- **Exercise.** Practice gentle exercise and stretching to build up stamina and energy.

- **Meditate.** Meditation increases endorphins, which are the natural painkillers, and reduces stress hormones.

- **Get a blood test to measure your cortisol level.** If your cortisol level is low, consider temporary natural cortisol replacement per your physician's recommendation.

- **Rest a lot.** Sleep is healing and restorative.

- **Take B vitamins daily.**

- **Take 2,000–5,000 mg of vitamin C daily in the acute phase.**

- **Consider IV vitamin C drips of 10,000–25,000 mg.** This will increase your energy level and immunity and support adrenal health. Holistic physicians often offer this treatment. I get one to strengthen my immune system when I'm coming down with a cold.

- **Eliminate the energy vampires in your life.** Try to rid yourself of toxic people or at least set clear limits and boundaries so they don't sap you. You can learn more in chapter 5.

4. The Three-Minute Heart Meditation

To counter emotional or physical distress, act fast by getting out of the immediate toxic situation to take a short break with this three-minute meditation. You can practice this almost anywhere—at home, at work, in the bathroom at parties, or on a park bench.

Close your eyes. Take a few deep breaths and relax. Then place your palm over your heart chakra, in the middle of your chest. Focus on a beautiful image that you love: a sunset, a rose, the ocean, a child's face. Feel the love building in your heart and throughout your body. Let this loving feeling soothe you. Toxic energy leaves your body when you become purified with love. For just three-minute bursts throughout the day, you can meditate on the loving-kindness in your heart and feel that energy clear away stress.

You can send this loving-kindness to specific areas of your body too. My most vulnerable point is my gut. If I sense that I've taken on someone else's symptom, I place my hand over my belly and send it loving-kindness. This dissolves my discomfort. What is your most sensitive point? Is it your neck? Do you get bladder infections? Headaches? Send these areas loving-kindness to clear away toxic energy so it doesn't lodge there.

Sometimes it's easier to meditate on the well-being of someone else (which opens your heart too) rather than yourself. Do this if you're having a hard time meditating on yourself.

5. Meditation for Loving Your Empath Body

Your body is a temple that houses your spirit, so it's vital that you regard it as a friend, a sacred place, and a receptacle for intuition. Your body is not an enemy. The following meditation will help you

commit to fully inhabiting your body so that you can be more pres-
ent and joyous.

Find time for solitude in a beautiful space. Don't force the mind
to quiet but rather shift channels. Take a few deep breaths. Feel
each inhalation and exhalation. Slow yourself down so that you
can be more aware of your body. Let any negative thoughts
float by while you return to your breath, the sacred prana. Feel
its motion bring you into your deeper self. Settle your energy
within the bounds of your body, cells, and organs.

Become aware of your toes. Wiggle them and note the beautiful feeling of awakening the feet. Next, bring your awareness
to your ankles. As you continue breathing, move your focus
up your legs to your knees. Then continue to bring your attention up to your strong thighs, and note how grounded they
feel. Inwardly thank them for holding you up. Then bring
your awareness to your genitals and pelvic area. Many women
experience clenching here. You might want to inwardly say, "I
recognize you. I'm not turning my back on you anymore. I'm
going to learn about you and love you. You are part of me."

Move your awareness now to your belly. Are you holding
any tension, burning, or other discomfort there? This is the
chakra where we process emotions. Soothe and heal this area
by bringing loving awareness to your belly. Focus on your chest
now, where your heart chakra resides, the center for unconditional love. Make it your friend so you can be loving to yourself.
Feel a shower of positive energy coursing through your heart.
Return here often to feel the nurturing energy. Now, expand
this awareness to your shoulders, arms, wrists, and beautiful
hands. Feel and move each finger. These are all an extension of
the heart chakra.

Next, bring your attention to your neck. The communication chakra resides in the throat area. Notice if you feel any tension here that would stop you from expressing yourself. Send love to this area.

Now, bring your awareness to your head, feeling your beautiful face, your ears, mouth, eyes, nose, and third eye, which resides between your eyebrows. This is the center for intuition. You might see swirling purple colors in your mind's eye as you tune in. Finally, bring your attention to the top of your head. This is the crown chakra, the center for white light, your connection to Spirit. Feel the inspiration that emanates from here.

When you are ready to conclude this meditation, inwardly say "thank you" for the experience of feeling present in your body. Affirm to yourself, "I am ready to come into my full power as an embodied empath." Take a few deep breaths. Then slowly and gently open your eyes. Return fully to your environment, more aware of your body than ever.

6. Tips to Prevent Empathy Overload and to Decompress

The following are basic strategies that will help you deal with unwelcome energy. I use them in my life and teach them to my patients and workshop participants.

- **Inhale lavender essential oil.** You can also put a few drops midway between your eyebrows (on your third eye) to calm yourself.

- **Be in nature.**

- **Manage your time wisely.** Balance your alone time and people time. Time management is key to my sanity. I try not to schedule patients back to back, and in my personal life, I don't plan too many things in one day. I've also learned to cancel plans when I get overloaded. This is a skill all empaths must learn so we don't feel obligated to go out when we're tired and need rest.

- **Set clear limits with energy vampires and toxic people.** Remember that "no" is a complete sentence. You don't have to keep explaining yourself. I am adamant about avoiding draining people, particularly when I'm overloaded.

- **Practice self-compassion.** Be sweet to yourself whenever possible. Avoid beating yourself up. After a hard day, tell yourself, "I did the best I could. It's okay, honey."

- **Take a personal retreat, away from the world, at least once a year.** This is planned time to decompress in nature or another calming place so that you can wind down and recalibrate your system. Every year I offer a weekend retreat at Esalen Institute among the gorgeous redwoods and above the Pacific Ocean in Big Sur, California. It's a time for participants to slow down, tune in to their intuition, and reconnect to their spirits more deeply. I also take a few personal retreats in nature every year to restore myself.

7. Open to a Higher Power

If you're about to pick up a drink, overeat, or engage in another addiction, stop for a few minutes. Remember that the secret to overcoming cravings and anxiety is to shift out of your addicted small self and into your spiritual power. Practice the following exercise to tune in to your higher power. It can take you from an overwhelmed state of mind into a much larger state of consciousness, where you don't need to numb your sensitivities to feel okay.

For at least five minutes every day, pause from your busy life and cease all problem solving so that you can connect to your higher power. Sit in a tranquil space, whether at home, in a park, in nature, or even in your office with the door closed. Then breathe deeply and slowly to relax your body. When thoughts come, picture them as clouds floating in the sky, coming and going. Do not attach to them. Keep returning to the rhythm of your breath.

Spirit is energy. Once you're in a relaxed state, inwardly invite in the presence of Spirit—however you name it. First look within yourself, where Spirit is easier to sense. Feel Spirit in your heart and in your body. Don't overthink this. Sense the warmth of love opening your heart and beginning to flow throughout your body. Feel your higher power. Really get an energetic sense of it. Savor this sensation. No rush. No pressure. Take time to let in the beautiful feeling. Once you get a sense of what your higher power feels like, you can easily reconnect with it again and again.

In this state, you can also ask for help from Spirit. For instance, "Please help me not absorb the anger of my bullying boss," or "Please lift my anxiety in social situations," or "Please help my partner understand my sensitivities." For optimal results, focus on one request per meditation. This makes the request more potent and lets you track the results.

To conclude, say an inward "thank you" to Spirit, and take a small bow in reverence to honor this experience. Then slowly and gently open your eyes.

8. Keep a Meditation Pillow in Front of Your Refrigerator

Practice the following strategy to ward off the desire to overeat when you're stressed and want to protect yourself from negativity.

Keep a meditation pillow in front of your refrigerator. When the urge to overeat strikes, this visual cue can stop you from opening that refrigerator door. It is a tangible reminder to meditate to ground yourself. Instead of reaching for food, sit on the pillow and close your eyes. Breathe deeply to stabilize yourself energetically. Now, compassionately ask yourself what triggered the impulse to eat. Was it a rude boss? A feeling of anxiety? Did going to a shopping mall exhaust you? Inwardly try to pinpoint the cause. Be gentle with yourself. When obsessive thoughts to eat intrude, picture the energy of love flooding your body from head to toe. Let the divine sense of love that is dissolving your fears and insecurities satiate you. Love can feel warm, and it nourishes your soul and your body. Keep tuning in to this feeling of self-soothing. Tell yourself there is nothing to be afraid of. You have the power to stabilize your own energy through meditation. Take another deep breath, exhale completely, and know that all is well.

9. Define and Express Your Relationship Needs

Knowing your needs and being able to assert them is a strong form of self-protection for empaths. Then we can be in our full power in a relationship. If something doesn't feel right, raise the issue with the person rather than suffering silently. Finding your voice is equivalent to finding your power. Without it, you may become exhausted, anxious, and can feel like a doormat in relationships where your basic needs are unmet. Most people are not mind readers. Speak up to safeguard your well-being. The following strategy will support you in this.

Quiet your mind with slow and regular breaths. Feel the joy of having this time to listen to your deepest self. When you feel relaxed and receptive, inwardly ask yourself these questions: What do I need in a relationship that I've been afraid to ask for? Which of my sensitivities would I most like another to support? What would make me feel most comfortable with this person? Pose any other questions that arise for you. Then intuitively tune in to the answers rather than trying to figure them out. Listen to your body and its signals. Let aha! feelings and intuitive insights flow. Take special note of those that make you feel more powerful and protected.

Stay open. Don't censor anything. Would you prefer more alone or quiet time? With a partner, would you like to sleep by yourself sometimes? Do you want to play more, talk more, or have sex more with your partner? Would you like to dance under the full moon together? Let your intuition flow without judgment. Uncover your true feelings. There is no reason to be ashamed or to hold back.

Focus on treasuring your needs as an empath. Compassionately accept all your quirks and sensitivities. Let this loving feeling inspire you to be authentically you. By defining what does and doesn't feel good for you, you're honoring yourself and keeping negative energy out. When you feel complete with this inquiry, sit quietly for a few moments, immersed in good feelings.

10. Observe the No-Yelling Rule

Yelling and loud voices overwhelm empaths. Observe the no-yelling rule in your home and set limits with people who dump anger. Our partners and friends need to accept that they can't yell around us. For the sake of self-preservation, I'm strict about this rule in my house. People can express anger in a healthy way without yelling. One empath told me, "I cannot stand arguing around me. The vibration of anger in my body feels like I'm being hit. If I'm in a yelling match, I'm drained for days." Also, avoid arguing around children because they often feel that they're the cause of the conflict.

11. Protect Yourself from Narcissists

Narcissists act as if the world revolves around them. They have a grandiose sense of importance and entitlement and require endless praise. They can also be extremely intuitive, but they use their intuition to manipulate and achieve their goals. Use the following strategies to protect yourself from them:

- **Lower your expectations of their emotional capabilities.**

- **Don't let yourself be manipulated.**

- **Don't expect them to respect your sensitivities because they are extremely cold people.**

- **Don't fall in love with a narcissist.** Run in the opposite direction no matter how attracted you feel.

- **Try to avoid working with a narcissistic boss.**
  If you can't leave, don't let your self-esteem
  depend on your boss's reactions.

- **The only way to get through to a narcissist is to
  stroke their ego.** Frame your requests in terms of
  how they can benefit from them. For instance, if you
  want to take a few days off to attend a work-related
  conference, say something like, "This will help me
  make your business more successful," rather than, "I
  could use a break from the office." To successfully
  communicate and get the results you desire, show
  how your request will be to the narcissist's advantage.

- **To end a relationship with a narcissist (or anyone
  with whom you want a complete break), go cold
  turkey.** Stop all contact and never look back. In
  addition, you can use the following cord-cutting
  visualization and a shamanic technique for
  honorable closure.

  ▲ **Practice a cord-cutting visualization.** In a calm
  state, picture cords of light connecting both of you.
  Inwardly say "thank you" for what you've learned
  from the relationship, even if the lessons were hard.
  Then firmly assert, "It's time to completely break
  our bonds." Next, visualize taking a pair of scissors
  and cutting each bond completely so that you're
  free of any energetic ties. This visualization will
  help you release the relationship and also remove
  lingering energy that you feel from the person.

▲ **Have honorable closure.** This shamanic technique lets you release a relationship, particularly if you keep thinking about the person or sense that they're thinking about you. Go out into nature and find a large stick. Look at the stick and declare, "This relationship is over." Then break the stick in half, leave the pieces on the ground, walk away, and never look back. This finalizes the ceremony of closure.

12. Protect Yourself from Rageaholics

Rageaholics deal with conflict by accusing, attacking, and controlling, and often yell to make a point. They usually behave most poorly around their loved ones. Use the following strategies to protect yourself from them:

• **Let the rageaholic know that you hear them.** Then suggest that you work the issue out respectfully when they calm down. Say something like, "I want to help you, but it's hard for me to listen when you're in this state." Refuse to engage with their anger.

• **Set a no-yelling rule.** It's just not allowed around you. There are other ways to resolve conflicts without yelling.

• **Stay calm.** Do not yell back when triggered. Reacting impulsively will just drain you and aggravate the situation.

• **If the person won't stop yelling, leave the room or ask the person to leave.**

- **Pause when you're agitated.** Take a timeout to quiet the fight-or-flight response. Count to ten or take some time alone if necessary. Wait until you're calm to respond to someone's anger; otherwise, the person may dump more of it on you.

- **Practice restraint of speech, which includes texting, email, and the phone.** Then you'll be in charge of your emotions when you choose to address the person.

13. Protect Yourself from Victims

People with a victim mentality drain empaths with their "the world is against me" attitude. They don't take responsibility for the difficulties in their lives. Empaths often fall into the compassionate caretaker role with people who portray themselves as victims, trying to help them solve their problems. Use the following suggestions to assert boundaries with these people. Do not become codependent and fall into the trap of becoming their caretaker or therapist.

- **Set compassionate and clear boundaries.** People hear us better when we're not being snippy.

- **Use the Three-Minute Phone Call.** This entails listening briefly and then telling your friend or family member, "I support you, but I can only listen for a few minutes if you keep rehashing the same issues. Perhaps you'd like to find a therapist to help you."

- **Say "no" with a smile.** With a coworker, smile and say something like, "I'll hold positive thoughts for the best possible outcome. Thank you for understanding that I must get back to work." With friends and family, briefly empathize with their problem, and then say "no" by pleasantly changing the subject. Do not encourage their complaining.

- **Set limits with body language.** This is a good time to cross your arms and break eye contact to send the message that you're busy and not going to indulge them.

14. Protect Yourself from Drama Queens and Kings

Drama queens and kings drain sensitive people by overloading us with too much information and stimulation. They are energized when we react to their drama, but if we remain calm, they don't get rewarded. Be consistent. Then they will lose interest and go on to the next person. Here are a few specific guidelines:

- **Don't ask these people how they are doing.** You don't want to know.

- **If a drama queen or king does start up, breathe deeply and stay calm.** Do not get caught in their story.

- **Set kind but firm limits.** For example, to a friend who keeps canceling plans with you because of one drama after another, you can say something like, "I'm sorry for all your mishaps, but let's not reschedule until things settle down for you and you can show up." This way, you will be communicating clearly and won't be reinforcing their behavior.

15. Protect Yourself from Control Freaks and Critics

Control freaks and critics feel qualified to offer their unsolicited opinion and proceed to tell you, whether or not you want to hear their advice. Ongoing unwelcome advice like this is draining for empaths. Use the following suggestions to protect yourself from this kind of dynamic:

* **Be assertive.** Don't tell these types what to do. This will only make them defensive. Tell them something like, "Thanks for your advice, but I want to think about how to approach this situation for myself."

* **Politely ask the person to stop criticizing you.** Be firm but not emotional. Don't play the victim.

* **Stay aware.** If you notice that you feel inadequate around this person, identify the self-esteem issues that have been triggered and work on healing them. The more secure you feel, the less these vampires can hurt you.

16. Protect Yourself from Nonstop Talkers

Nonstop talkers can drain the life force out of others, especially empaths. We are incredible listeners and often make the mistake of tolerating nonstop talkers for far too long. Then we become exhausted. Use the following strategies to protect yourself:

- **Nonstop talkers don't respond to nonverbal cues.**
  These include looking impatient or restless. You
  must interrupt them, as hard as this may be to do.

- **Although you may feel like saying, "Be quiet
  because you're driving me crazy," that will only
  make the talker defensive or angry.** Instead,
  smile and nicely excuse yourself. You might say,
  "Please pardon me for interrupting, but I need to
  talk to someone else at the party," or "I have an
  appointment I must keep." A socially acceptable
  reason to leave that I often use is "I have to go to
  the bathroom."

- **Express yourself in a neutral and nonblaming
  tone.** For example, you can say, "I'd like to add to
  the discussion too. It would be great if you would
  let me contribute." If you communicate without
  irritation, you are more likely to be heard.

- **Use humor.** For example, with people you know
  well, you can jokingly say, "The clock is ticking,"
  as one good friend does with me when I get
  long-winded.

17. Protect Yourself from Passive-Aggressive People

*Passive-aggressive people express their anger with a smile instead of
yelling. They sugarcoat hostility and send confusing messages, but
empaths can intuitively sense the anger beneath the pleasant facade.
Here are some strategies to protect yourself from this behavior:*

- **Trust yourself.** Don't question your response to them, because their anger is hidden. Trust your intuition.

- **Recognize the pattern and address the behavior.**

- **Focus on one issue at a time so that the person doesn't feel attacked.** For instance, if a friend keeps saying "yes" when you ask for help but doesn't follow through, you can say in a neutral tone: "Please don't make a commitment if you can't follow through." Then notice how the person responds. They might say, "I apologize. I have to be more focused." Then, see if their behavior changes. If it doesn't, you can raise the issue with them again or simply accept that they're not dependable and stop making any further requests.

- **If you can't get a direct answer from the person, ask them to clarify their position.** It's important to address the behavior and find a solution. Being specific with someone who is passive-aggressive will make them take a stand.

18. How to Cure an Emotional Hangover

Despite your best efforts, it's not uncommon to experience an "emotional hangover," an energetic residue left over from interactions with energy vampires. Toxic emotions can linger long afterward, making you feel exhausted or ill or beset with brain fog. You may need time to recuperate. Try the following suggestions for your emotional hangover:

- **Practice the shower meditation.** While you're standing under the stream of water in your shower, say this affirmation: "Let this water wash all the negative energy from my body, mind, and spirit." Feel the shower cleansing you, making you clean, fresh, positive, and rejuvenated.

- **Use gemstones.** Carry a crystal to help ground you and ward off an emotional hangover. Try black tourmaline, amethyst, or black obsidian. Shamans say that if you carry or wear black, you will be more protected.

- **Smudge your space.** In Native American culture, burning medicinal and aromatic plants clears negative or stagnant energy from a location. This technique is called "smudging." I love to burn sweetgrass. Its beautiful smell wafting through the air feels nurturing to my feminine energy. Sage is another popular and effective choice. I also like to pick cypress, eucalyptus, and juniper sprigs to burn. Experiment with the plant scents that you like.

- **Use negative ion generators or salt lamps.** These devices produce negative ions, which clear the air of dust, mold spores, pollen, odors, cigarette smoke, bacteria, and viruses. They are also believed to remove negative energy from a space. The stream of moving water in the shower also produces negative ions.

- **Light a white candle.** This sets a meditative mood while also removing unpleasant energy from the environment. White contains all colors of the spectrum and creates a feeling of comfort and calm.

- **Spray rosewater or use other scents from aromatherapy.** The delicate scent of rosewater is lovely. I find it effective in removing an emotional hangover. A nice way to benefit from the scent of an essential oil is to use an aromatherapy diffuser, which spreads the scent throughout the air. Try lavender, spearmint, juniper, sage, frankincense, or myrrh, and experience the sublime scent purifying your energy and the room. Avoid synthetic oils because they contain toxic ingredients.

- **Get out in nature.** Hug a tree. Connect to the earth with your bare feet on the ground. Rejoice in the flowers. Hold a rock in your hand. Breathe in fresh air to cure an emotional hangover. The purity of nature can restore your clarity and uplift your mood.

- **Create a sacred space for meditation.** Place candles, incense, flowers, or a statue of a holy figure such as Quan Yin, the goddess of compassion, on a table in a quiet corner. Meditating in a sacred space builds positive energy and is a balm for an emotional hangover.

- **Seek emotional support.** If you feel negativity lingering from a toxic interaction, say from a narcissistic boss or a critical spouse, you may need some extra help to remove it. Talking out the situation with a friend or a therapist will allow you to voice and dispel the remaining negativity.

19. A Meditation for Mothers: Feeling the Goddess Within

I recommend that mothers, including pregnant mothers, use the following meditation daily to reap the serene spiritual, emotional, and physical benefits of endorphins. This meditation also creates a protective bubble of positive energy.

Take five minutes to breathe slowly and deeply. As you do so, put your hand on your heart and flood yourself with love and appreciation for who you are as a mother. Experience the warmth, connection, blessing, and gratitude of being a parent. Mothers are goddesses of creation. Maternal nurturing is an act of deep love. Feel the power of the mother goddess within you. She is the part of you that is connected to the earth and all the natural cycles in a profound and mystical way. In ancient times, the mother goddess was worshipped by many cultures. Feel her primal power within you, and hail her presence in your being.

20. Help Your Children Turn the Dial Down on Stress

Teach your empath child the following visualization to break the cycle of stress when they're feeling too much coming at them. They can use it anywhere—at home, at school, and with their friends. This technique is a part of the basic tool kit for all empathic children.

Here's what you say to your child: In your imagination, picture a big dial on a table in front of you. It has numbers on it, and they go from 10 on the left side to zero on the right side. Currently, this dial is set at ten. See yourself slowly turning the setting on the dial down, starting with 10. Turn the dial clockwise to the right, as the numbers get smaller and smaller, until you reach zero: 10, 9, 8, 7, 6, 5, 4, 3, 2, and 1. As you turn the dial this way, feel yourself getting more and more relaxed. You are lowering your stress and discomfort. When you reach zero, you will feel calm and happy.

If your child is too young to imagine this dial, you can draw a picture of it and have them point to their stress level. Then slowly count down with them until you reach zero.

21. Set Energetic Boundaries at Work

Empaths often suffer at work because they absorb the stress in their surroundings. The workplace can be noisy and overstimulating. The following suggestions will help you protect your energy in an emotionally demanding or crowded environment. They will create a cocoon of protection you can rely on.

- **If you are in an open space or chaotic office,** surround the outer edge of your desk with plants or photos of family or pets to create a psychological barrier.

- **Sacred objects, such as a statue of Quan Yin,** St. Francis, or the Buddha, as well as sacred beads or crystals can set an energetic boundary.

- **Pause.** Take bathroom breaks for relief, or walk outside in the fresh air.

- **Noise-canceling earbuds or headphones are useful** for muffling conversations and unwelcome sounds.

- **Visualize.** Picture a golden egg of light surrounding your workstation to repel negativity. You are always safe and protected within the golden egg.

22. How Therapists Can Stop Taking on Patients' Emotions

How do empaths pursue their calling as healers and therapists without taking on a patient's symptoms? The following suggestions will help you stay centered and clear. All healthcare professionals can benefit from adopting them to their work too.

- **Adjust your attitude.** Don't become a martyr. Your role is to be a guide for your patients, not to take on their pain or remove it. When you're clear about this, you'll enjoy your work more and excel at it.

- **Identify three obvious differences between you and your patient.** A good intellectual way to distance yourself from a patient's emotions and pain after a session is to focus on three clear differences between you. For example, I'm a woman, and he's a man. She's depressed, but I'm not. I'm a vegan, and he eats meat. This lets you appreciate what's you and

what's the patient, a boundary that helps prevent
you from absorbing unwanted energy.

- **Don't try to fix others.** People heal themselves. You
can support your patients' healing, but they must
make the necessary changes to free themselves
from suffering.

- **Watch out for codependency.** Be careful not to
get hooked into feeling responsible for someone's
progress. People change on their own timeline,
not yours. Of course, your heart will go out to
patients who are emotionally stuck or backsliding.
Guide them as much as possible, but you are not
responsible for their growth or their ability to
overcome obstacles.

- **Work on your own issues.** We tend to absorb
energy that is related to issues we haven't resolved
in ourselves. Compassionately notice when your
patients push your own emotional buttons. Ask
yourself, "Is this patient mirroring issues in
me that need healing?" Identify your triggers.
Depression? Fear of abandonment? Fear of
rejection? Anxiety about health? Intimacy? Focus
on healing those triggers and issues in yourself.
Then you won't be as susceptible to absorbing these
from others. Peer-oriented supervision groups
where you can present cases and discuss what
emotionally triggers you are helpful, as is working
with your own therapist.

23. The Jaguar Protection Meditation

I recommend the following meditation to call on the power of the jaguar to protect you. I use it when I need extra protection, especially if too much negativity is coming at me too fast. The jaguar is a fierce and patient guardian that can keep toxic energy and people away.

Find a quiet environment where you can't be interrupted. Sit in a comfortable position, and take a few deep breaths to center yourself and let go of stress. In this calm state, from deep within your heart, call on the spirit of the jaguar to protect you. Feel its presence enter. Then visualize this gorgeous, powerful creature patrolling your energy field, encircling it, protecting you, and keeping intruders and any negative forces that want to get through out. Picture what the jaguar looks like—its beautiful, fierce, and loving eyes; its sleek body; the graceful and purposeful way it moves. Feel secure in the circle of its protection.

As you close this meditation, give inner thanks to the jaguar. Know that you can call on it whenever there is a need. Feel the power of that. Then slowly and gently open your eyes. Orient yourself back to current time and space. Completely return to your own body, and be alert, aware, and present in your environment.

24. Tips to Protect Yourself from Intuitive Overload

The wonder of being an intuitive empath is that you're open to exploring realms beyond the linear one. The challenge, though, is not to get overwhelmed by too much information. By grounding, centering, and staying humble about your gifts, you will be better able to use them to everyone's benefit.

- **Dialogue with your inner voice.** You can always ask your inner voice to slow down so that you can take a break or find a rhythm that's more comfortable. Intuition doesn't just happen to us. You can cultivate an active and conscious connection with it.

- **Develop a witness state.** When you tune in, try to stay neutral. In many situations, the role of an empath is simply to bear witness—a sacred duty that the ancient prophets understood. You might wonder: Why am I sensing death, illness, or other painful circumstances at all? What good is it if I can't prevent them? Keep in mind that the act of *seeing* in itself bears light. Sometimes it's not your job to intervene, nor is it possible. In those situations, you can always hold the light for people. This is a holy act that supports others in miraculous ways.

- **You are not responsible for the karma of others.** Keep reminding yourself that everyone deserves the dignity of walking their own path. This will help you avoid feeling inappropriately responsible for what you intuitively sense.

- **Visualize light.** Picture divine white light coming though the crown of your head as darkness flows out the bottom of your feet. This process reduces overwhelm by circulating positive energy into your body and releasing toxic energy.

CREATING COMMUNITY
Setting Up Your Own Empath Support Group

E mpaths flourish around other sensitive and loving people, who can "see" and understand them. Having a community of kindred souls helps us survive and thrive. Whether your community is made up of a few people or more, this circle of mutual support can help everyone's sensitivities grow, uplift each of you in difficult times, and make it safer to open your hearts to experience more joy.

GUIDELINES FOR CREATING AN EMPATH SUPPORT GROUP

- **Membership.** Decide whether the group will be by invitation only or open to the public.

- **Location.** It's best to meet in a private home, a conference room in a quiet building, or a quiet area in a park.

- **Length and frequency of group.** Check with the members to see what works best, whether that's sixty to ninety minutes weekly, bimonthly, or monthly.

- **Size of group.** This can be anywhere from two to fifty people or more. Decide whether you want to limit the group to a certain size.

- **Formulate a short mission statement.** State that the purpose of the group is to focus on empath issues and solutions rather than turning the meeting into a pity party. You can find an example of a mission statement on my website, drjudithorloff.com, under "Empath Support."

- **Recommended reading and audio material.** *The Empath's Survival Guide* and/or the companion audio program, *Essential Tools for Empaths: A Survival Guide for Sensitive People.* In addition, you can include material from the selected reading list at the end of this book.

SUGGESTED FORMAT OF A MEETING

Option 1

- A member volunteers to be the group leader, committing to this role for one to six months.

- Prior to each meeting, the leader invites a speaker from within or outside the group to share their experiences and solutions as a sensitive person.

- The leader welcomes everyone to the meeting and reads the mission statement to the group.

- The members have a two-minute group meditation or silent period to decompress and become fully present.

- The speaker reads a selection of about three pages from *The Empath's Survival Guide,* or the speaker plays a selected section from the audio program *Essential Tools for Empaths* for the group. Next, the speaker discusses the topic for ten minutes.

- Then the meeting is opened for sharing on the topic. Limit the sharing to three to five minutes per person, with no crosstalk.

- After the sharing, allow five minutes for the group to practice an exercise or meditation from the book or audio program.

- To end the meeting, the leader selects a member to read an empath affirmation they like from the book.

Option 2

Create an Empath Study Group. Prior to each meeting, participants read the same section from *The Empath's Survival Guide* or listen to a portion of *Essential Tools for Empaths* audio program. The group meets to discuss the selection.

ACKNOWLEDGMENTS

I am grateful to the many people who support my writing and my sensitivities as an empath. Richard Pine, my extraordinary literary agent and champion of my work. Susan Golant, my skilled, patient, and devoted editor. Rhonda Bryant, my goddess assistant, sounding board, friend, and shaman. Corey Folsom, my loving partner, ally, and confidant. Berenice Glass, my friend and mirror, who keeps helping me love and grow in deeper ways. Lorin Roche and Camille Maurine, friends and fellow writers: I love playing with you and walking together on the beach, just enjoying and loving one another.

A special thanks to the fantastic team at Sounds True: Tami Simon, Haven Iverson, Jennifer Brown, Mitchell Clute, Wendy Gardner, Kira Roark, Sarah Gorecki, Christine Day, and Gretchen Gordon.

In addition, I offer deep appreciation to friends and family for their inspiration, personal stories, and contributions to this book. Ron Alexander, Margo Anand, Barbara Baird, Jim Benson, Barbara Biziou, Ann Buck, Laurie Sue Brockway, Ram Dass, Lily and David Dulan, Felice Dunas, Peter Erskine, Susan Foxley, Victor Fuhrman, Pamela Kaplan, Laura Greenberg, Sandra Ingerman, Reggie Jordan, Mignon McCarthy, Dean Orloff, Maxine Orloff, Meg McLaughlin-Wong, Cathy Lewis, Liz Olson, Dr. Richard Metzner, Charlotte Reznick, Al Saenz, Rabbi Don Singer, Leong Tan, Josh Touber, and Mary Williams.

I am indebted to my patients and workshop participants, from whom I continue to learn so much. I have disguised their names and identifying characteristics to protect their privacy. Also, I want to thank the nearly six thousand members of my Facebook Empath Support Community, who courageously embrace themselves as empaths and use their sensitivities to create good in their lives and the world.

NOTES

CHAPTER 1

1. "Sensitive? Emotional? Empathetic? It Could Be in Your Genes," Stony Brook Newsroom (June 2014): sb.cc.stonybrook.edu/news/medical/140623empatheticAron.php.

2. Lea Winerman, "The Mind's Mirror," *American Psychological Association Monitor on Psychology* 36, no. 4 (October 2005): 48, apa.org/monitor/oct05/mirror.aspx.

3. Rollin McCraty, Mike Atkinson, Dana Tomasino, Raymond Trevor Bradley, "The Coherent Heart: Heart-Brain Interactions, Psychophysiological Coherence, and the Emergence of System-Wide Order," *Integral Review* 5, no. 2 (December 2009): heartmathbenelux.com/doc/McCratyeal_article_in_integral_review_2009.pdf.

4. Elaine Hatfield, Richard L. Rapson, Yen-Chi L. Le, "Emotional Contagion and Empathy," *The Social Neuroscience of Empathy* (March 2009): doi:10.7551/mitpress/9780262012973.003.0003.

5. Thomas Levy, "Altering Brain Chemistry Makes Us More Sensitive to Inequality," *Berkeley News* (March 2015): news.berkeley.edu/2015/03/19/dopamine-inequality/.

6. Michael J Banissy, Jamie Ward, "Mirror-Touch Synesthesia Is Linked with Empathy," *Nature Neuroscience* 10 (2007): 815–816, nature.com/neuro/journal/v10/n7/full/nn1926.html; Thomas J. Palmeri, Randolph B. Blake, Ren Marois, "What is synesthesia?" *Scientific American* (June 2002): scientificamerican.com/article/what-is-synesthesia/.

CHAPTER 2

1. Dominik Mischkowski, Jennifer Crocker, Baldwin M. Way, "From Painkiller to Empathy Killer: Acetaminophen (Paracetamol) Reduces Empathy for Pain," *Oxford Journals: Cognitive and Affective Neuroscience* (May 2016): doi:10.1093/scan/nsw057.

CHAPTER 6

1. Erika M. Manczak, Anita DeLongis, Edith Chen, "Does Empathy Have a Cost? Diverging Psychological and Physiological Effects within Families," *Health Psychology* 35, no. 3 (March 2016): 211–218, doi:10.1037/hea0000281.

2. Sarina M. Rodrigues, Laura R. Saslow, Natalia Garcia, Oliver P. John, Dacher Keltner, "Oxytocin Receptor Genetic Variation Relates to Empathy and Stress Reactivity in Humans," *Proceedings of the National Academy of Sciences* 105, no. 50 (December 2009): 21437–21441, doi:10.1073/pnas.0909579106.

3. Diana Divecha, "Is Empathy Learned—Or Are We Born with It?" *Developmental Science* (December 2012): developmentalscience.com/blog/2012/12/02/is-empathy-learned-or-are-we-born-with-it; Alison Gopnik,"'Empathic Civilization': Amazing Empathic Babies," The Huffington Post (April 2010): huffingtonpost.com/alison-gopnik/empathic-civilization-ama_b_473961.html; Daniel Goleman, "Researchers Trace Empathy's Roots to Infancy," *New York Times* (March 1989): nytimes.com/1989/03/28/science/researchers-trace-empathy-s-roots-to-infancy.html?pagewanted=all.

4. Janet L. Hopson, "Fetal Psychology: Your Baby Can Feel, Dream, and Even Listen to Mozart in the Womb," *Psychology Today* (September 1998): psychologytoday.com/articles/199809/fetal-psychology.

5. Janet A. DiPietro, Sterling C. Hilton, Melissa Hawkins, Kathleen A. Costigan, Eva K. Pressman, "Maternal Stress and Affect Influence Fetal Neurobehavioral Development," *Developmental Psychology* 38, no. 5 (September 2002): 659–668, doi:10.1037//0012-1649.38.5.659.

6. Tobias Grossmann, Tricia Striano, Angela D Friederici, "Infants' Electric Brain Responses to Emotional Prosody," *NeuroReport* 16, no. 16 (November 2005): 1825–1828, doi:10.1097/01.wnr.0000185964.34336.b1; Ashik Siddique, "Parents' Arguing in Front of Baby Alters Infant Brain Development," *Medical Daily* (March 2013): medicaldaily.com/parents-arguing-front-baby-alters-infant-brain-development-244769.

CHAPTER 7

1. Nora D. Volkow, Dardo Tomasi, Gene-Jack Wang, Paul Vaska, Joanna S. Fowler, Frank Telang, Dave Alexoff, Jean Logan, Christopher Wong, "Effects of Cell Phone Radio Frequency Signal Exposure on Brain Glucose Metabolism," *Journal of the American Medical Association* 305, no. 8 (February 2011): 808–813, doi:10.1001/jama.2011.186.

2. Elaine Hatfield, Richard L. Rapson, Yen-Chi L. Le, "Emotional Contagion and Empathy," *The Social Neuroscience of Empathy* (March 2009): doi:10.7551/mitpress/9780262012973.003.0003.

CHAPTER 8

1. Michael Forrester, "Increasing Solar Activity and Disturbances in Earth's Magnetic Field Affect Our Behavior and Increase Our Health," The Mind Unleashed (September 2014): themindunleashed.org/2014/09/increasing-solar-activity-disturbances-earths-magnetic-field-affect-behavior-increase-health.html; Jacqueline Marshall, "Solar Flare: The Sun Touches Our Psyche," *Washington Times* (March 2012): washingtontimes.com/news/2014/dec/31/solar-flare-sun-touches-our-psyche/; R.W. Kay, "Geomagnetic Storms: Association with Incidence of Depression as Measured by Hospital Admission," *The British Journal of Psychiatry* 164, no. 6 (March 1994): 403–409, doi:10.1192/bjp.164.3.403.

SELECTED READING

Aron, Elaine. *The Highly Sensitive Person: How to Thrive When the World Overwhelms You.* New York: Broadway Books, 1997.

Aron, Elaine. *The Highly Sensitive Person in Love: Understanding and Managing Relationships When the World Overwhelms You.* New York: Harmony, 2001.

Aron, Elaine. *The Highly Sensitive Child: Helping Our Children Thrive When the World Overwhelms Them.* New York: Harmony, 2002.

Beattie, Melody. *Codependent No More: How to Stop Controlling Others and Start Caring for Yourself.* Center City, MN: Hazelden, 1986.

Borba, Michele. *UnSelfie: Why Empathetic Kids Succeed in Our All-About-Me World.* New York: Touchstone, 2016.

Bradshaw, John. *Healing the Shame That Binds You.* Deerfield Beach, FL: Health Communications, 1988.

Cain, Susan. *Quiet: The Power of Introverts in a World That Can't Stop Talking.* New York: Broadway Books, 2013.

Chödrön, Pema. *When Things Fall Apart: Heart Advice for Difficult Times.* Boulder, CO: Shambhala Press, 1996.

Eden, Donna, and David Feinstein. *Energy Medicine: Balancing Your Body's Energies for Optimal Health, Joy, and Vitality.* The Penguin Group, 2008.

Naparstek, Belleruth. *Your Sixth Sense: Unlocking the Power of Your Intuition.* San Francisco: Harper One, 1997.

Ram Dass. *Be Here Now.* New York: Crown Publishing Group, 1971.

Salzberg, Sharon. *Lovingkindness: The Revolutionary Art of Happiness.* Boulder, CO: Shambhala Publications, 1995.

Tolle, Eckhart. *The Power of Now.* Vancouver, BC: Namaste Publishing, 1997.

Vitale, Joe and Hew Len, Ihaleakala. *Zero Limits: The Secret Hawaiian System for Wealth, Health, Peace, and More.* New York: Wiley, 2007.

Zeff, Ted. *The Strong, Sensitive Boy.* San Ramon, CA: Prana Publishing, 2010.

INDEX

addiction, 57–66
adrenal fatigue, 39–41, 217–18
affirmation mantras, 27, 56, 75, 105, 128, 161, 186, 206, 213
alone time, 46–47, 93–94, 134–35
animal empaths, 201–2
Aron, Elaine, 5
attachment, 80–81

Bach, Edward, 198
Butler, Kristen, 47

chi, 31
children who are empaths, 141–60
Chinese medicine, 31
chronos, 205–6
communication tips, 86–90, 97–98
control freaks and critics, 119–20, 231

diet and food issues, 66–74, 139–40
dopamine, 11
drama queens and kings, 118–19, 230
dream empaths, 193–95
dumping, 115

earth empaths, 198–201
Earthing and grounding, 24–26, 47, 200, 216–17
Einstein, Albert, 211
electromagnetic fields, 10
emotional contagion, 10–11, 168–69
emotional empaths, 32–35

ABOUT THE AUTHOR

Judith Orloff, MD, is a psychiatrist in private practice in Los Angeles and is on the psychiatric clinical faculty at UCLA. She specializes in treating highly sensitive people and empaths. Dr. Orloff, an empath herself, combines the pearls of conventional medical wisdom with cutting-edge knowledge of intuition, spirituality, and energy medicine. She is a *New York Times* bestselling author of *Emotional Freedom, The Power of Surrender, Positive Energy, Guide to Intuitive Healing, and Second Sight.* Her work has been featured on *The Today Show,* CNN, PBS, and in *USA Today* and *O, The Oprah Magazine.* To learn more about sensitive people, the power of intuition, or to join her Facebook Empath Support Community and empath newsletter, visit drjudithorloff.com.

ABOUT SOUNDS TRUE

Sounds True is a multimedia publisher whose mission is to inspire and support personal transformation and spiritual awakening. Founded in 1985 and located in Boulder, Colorado, we work with many of the leading spiritual teachers, thinkers, healers, and visionary artists of our time. We strive with every title to preserve the essential "living wisdom" of the author or artist. It is our goal to create products that not only provide information to a reader or listener, but that also embody the quality of a wisdom transmission.

For those seeking genuine transformation, Sounds True is your trusted partner. At SoundsTrue.com you will find a wealth of free resources to support your journey, including exclusive weekly audio interviews, free downloads, interactive learning tools, and other special savings on all our titles.

To learn more, please visit SoundsTrue.com/freegifts or call us toll-free at 800.333.9185.